3D Quilling

3D Quilling

How to Make 20 Decorative Flowers, Fruit, and More From Curled Paper Strips

Vaishali Rastogi Sahni

STACKPOLE
BOOKS

Guilford, Connecticut

STACKPOLE
BOOKS

Published by Stackpole Books
An imprint of The Rowman & Littlefield Publishing Group, Inc.
4501 Forbes Blvd., Ste. 200
Lanham, MD 20706
www.rowman.com

Distributed by NATIONAL BOOK NETWORK
800-462-6420

Text and Photography: Vaishali Rastogi Sahni
Editor: Julie Brooke
Design and Layout: Leah Germann

British Library Cataloguing in Publication Information available

Library of Congress Cataloging-in-Publication Data available

ISBN 978-0-8117-3786-9 (paperback)

∞™ The paper used in this publication meets the minimum requirements of American National Standard for Information Sciences—Permanence of Paper for Printed Library Materials, ANSI/NISO Z39.48-1992.

First Edition

Printed in China

Contents

Introduction

The art of quilling—rolling and curling strips of paper into shapes and then assembling them into patterns—has been around for centuries, and it is experiencing a revival today.

There is debate over where it began. Some people believe it started in ancient Egypt, and some forms of filigree art from this time have inspired modern quilling techniques. Or it may have been pioneered by French and Italian nuns during the Renaissance. They used strips of gilded paper, cut from the edges of books, to decorate book covers and religious items. In the eighteenth and nineteenth centuries, affluent women in Europe and North America decorated objects such as tea caddies, baskets, and jewelry boxes with quilling.

Today, new techniques and inexpensive materials have helped to make this craft increasingly popular, and it is enjoyed by people of all ages and from all walks of life. And you can do so much more than just make patterns with quilled paper! Why not use it to make spectacular three-dimensional figures?

I have always enjoyed arts and crafts. When I was at college, I saw an online video which featured beautiful flowers and designs made from paper strips. I instantly fell in love with the idea that simple strips of paper could be used to create unique and colorful designs. I was inspired! When I tried my hand at quilling, I discovered that I love doing it and creating three-dimensional works of art with it. I switched from a career in chartered accountancy to working full time in arts and crafts. Patience—which is the first requirement of quilling—has always been my strength. It enables me to create sculptures which can take weeks or months to complete. Although quilling is very time-consuming, I enjoy the beauty of each design and curl. Each time I create an artwork, it mesmerizes me. Quilling allows me to use colors with all their vibrancy and this in turn brings quilling closer to my heart.

Quilling tools (see page 118) are available from most craft stores and online. All you need to get started, and make most of the basic shapes, is a quilling tool, strips of paper, scissors, and glue. When you are ready to progress, you can buy additional tools, such as a needle tool, quilling comb, and paper cutter. Most projects require the same basic steps: quilling paper rolls and manipulating them into teardrops and petals, or shaping them into domes and cones using a Mini Mold; and making O-shapes. To make a three-dimensional object you should work in a logical order. For example, to make an animal, first create its face, then its body and limbs, and finally its facial features, hair, and tail.

Quilling is so satisfying to do and the results are spectacular—I hope you enjoy it as much as I do!

Vaishali Rastogi Sahni

Flowers

Delicate flower petals have always lent themselves to being reproduced in paper. Here, quilled paper is transformed into poppies, sunflowers, lotus, and chrysanthemum blooms. To complete the effect, just add paper leaves and wired stems.

Chrysanthemum

The chrysanthemum has been a sign of friendship and cheerfulness for generations, but this bloom has many meanings. In Japan—where it is a symbol of both the sun and the Emperor's family—it is celebrated with a festival of happiness. The chrysanthemum is grown in a variety of colors, but I have chosen the deep red flower that was a symbol of passion in the 19th century.

Getting started

First cut all your strips using a steel ruler and paper cutter on a cutting mat (see Techniques page 120). The flower has 192 petals which surround a sepal and sit on a base and stem.

- The first and second rows each contain twenty-four petals. For each petal you need one 1/32 x 11¾ in. (1 x 300mm) maroon paper strip
- The third, fourth, fifth, sixth and seventh rows each contain twenty-four petals. For each petal you will need one 1/24 x 23½ in. (1.5 x 600mm) maroon paper strip
- The eighth row contains twenty-four petals. For each petal you will need one 1/24 x 23½ in. (1.5 x 600mm) and one 1/24 x 11¾ in. (1.5 x 300mm) maroon paper strip
- For the sepal you need thirty-three 1/8 x 11¾ in. (3 x 300mm) and five ¾ x 11¾ in. (20 x 300mm) maroon paper strips
- For the base you need ten 1/16 x 11¾ in. (2 x 300mm) and eleven 1/24 x 11¾ in. (1.5 x 300mm) green paper strips

Note: You can use 1/24 in. (1.5mm) strips for the first and second rows if you find it difficult to handle 1/32 in. (1mm) strips. Join two 11¾ in. (300mm) strips to get 23½ in. (600mm) strips (see Techniques, page 121).

You will need

Maroon paper strips:
48 strips 1/32 x 11¾ in. (1 x 300mm)
144 strips 1/24 x 23½ in. (1.5 x 600mm)
24 strips 1/24 x 11¾ in. (1.5 x 300mm)
33 strips 1/8 x 11¾ in. (3 x 300mm)
5 strips ¾ x 11¾ in. (20 x 300mm)

Green paper strips:
10 strips 1/16 x 11¾ in. (2 x 300mm)
11 strips 1/24 x 11¾ in. (1.5 x 300mm)

Green taped wire for stem

Steel ruler
Paper cutter
Cutting mat
Quilling tool
Glue
Paintbrush
Sharp pair of scissors
Mini Mold
Paper clip
Paper cutting knife
Embossing pad
Embossing tool
Needle tool

Finished size

Approximately 3¼ in. (85mm) in diameter

Difficulty level

Moderate

Making the petals

1 For each petal in rows one (at the center of the flower) through seven (on the outside of the flower), take a strip measuring 1/32 x 11¾ in. or 1/24 x 23½ in. (1 x 300mm or 1.5 x 600mm). Make a tightly quilled roll and then slowly open the coils between your fingers until the gaps between the coils are almost equal (see Techniques page 122). Hold the center of the coil and push it to one side. Press the other side so that the petal forms a teardrop shape (see Techniques page 122).

2 Glue the end of the strip to secure it. Pinch the top of the petal. Repeat steps 1 and 2 to make 168 petals.

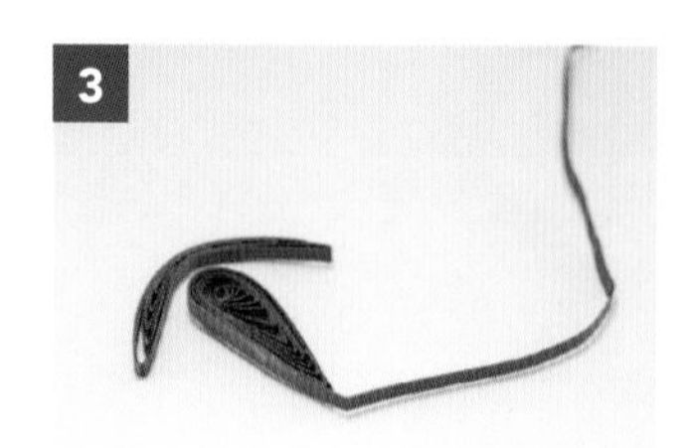

3 To make the petals for row eight, use one 1/24 x 23½ in. (1.5 x 600mm) strip to make a petal following steps 1 and 2. Now open out the last two coils and glue the strip at the bottom so that the rest of the petal does not open. Make an O-shape using a 1/24 x 11¾ in. (1.5 x 300mm) strip and glue it over the head of the petal. (See Techniques page 124 for how to make an O-shape).

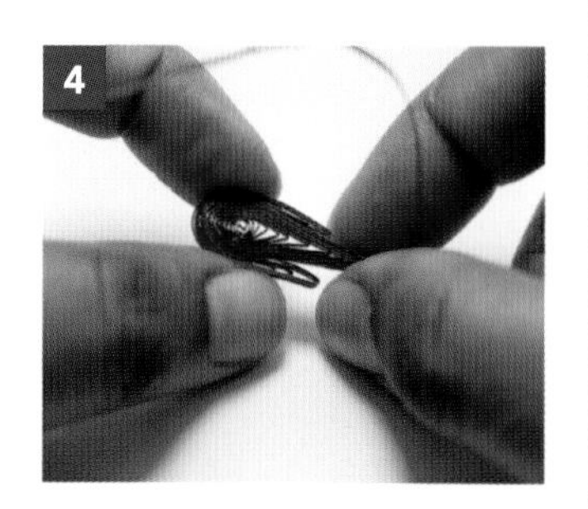

4 Wrap the edges of the O-shape around the teardrop using the leftover strip as shown in the photograph.

5 Apply glue to the back of five to six petals at a time (see Techniques page 119). Before the glue dries completely, but once it is no longer sticky and the petals are still malleable, use the Mini Mold to shape the top of each petal into a dome.

Assembling the petals

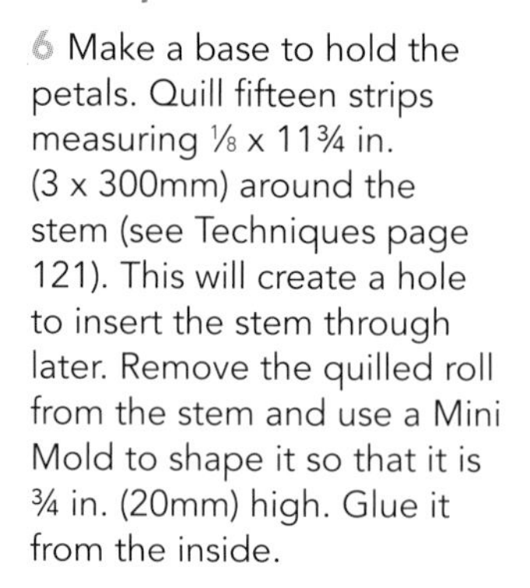

6 Make a base to hold the petals. Quill fifteen strips measuring 1/8 x 11¾ in. (3 x 300mm) around the stem (see Techniques page 121). This will create a hole to insert the stem through later. Remove the quilled roll from the stem and use a Mini Mold to shape it so that it is ¾ in. (20mm) high. Glue it from the inside.

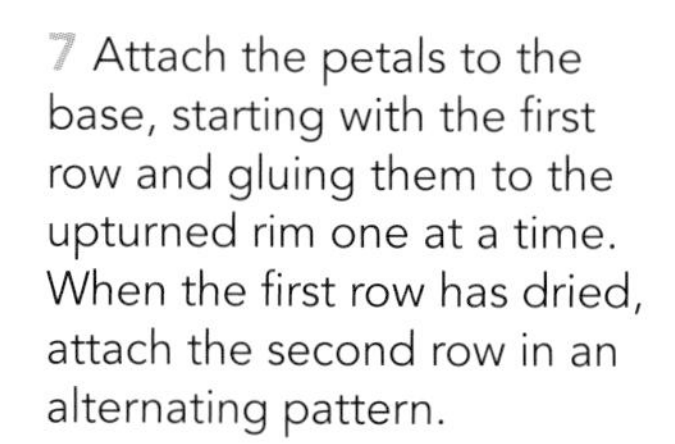

7 Attach the petals to the base, starting with the first row and gluing them to the upturned rim one at a time. When the first row has dried, attach the second row in an alternating pattern.

8 Attach the remaining rows of petals as before, fanning out the last row and arranging them to create a naturalistic effect. Let the glue dry completely.

Making the sepal

9 Use eighteen strips measuring ⅛ x 11¾ in. (3 x 300mm) to make two domes, each ½ in. (12mm) high; use eight-and-a-half strips for the first dome and nine-and-a-half for the second. Glue them on the inside and let dry completely. Place the smaller dome on top of the larger dome and glue them together to make a sphere.

10 Take five ¾ x 11¾ in. (20 x 300mm) strips. Use a paper cutting knife to cut curved spikes along one long edge of four of them. Hold the other long edge of the strip in a clip (see Techniques page 123). Use the same technique to cut rounded spikes into the fifth strip.

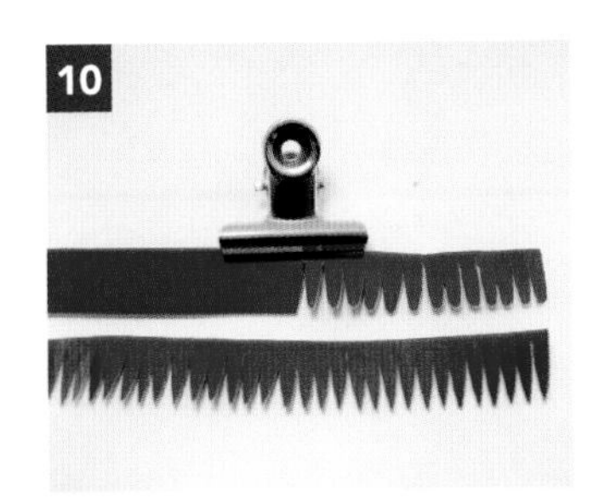

11 Use an embossing pad and tool to emboss the spikes to curve them (see Techniques page 124).

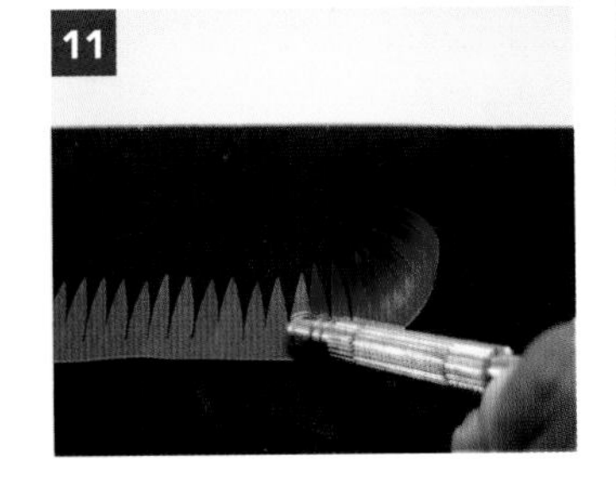

12 Use glue to attach the strips with curved spikes around the sphere. The tips of the first strip should reach the center of the top of the sphere. Attach the remaining curved-spike strips so that the tips sit just below those of the previous strip. Attach the fifth strip to the outside of the sphere.

Assembling the flower

13 Insert the stem through the hole in the dome. Make a small loop in the top of the stem so that it does not slide back through the hole, then glue it generously.

14 Use ten green strips measuring 1/16 x 11¾ in. (2 x 300mm) to make a dome ¼ in. (5mm) high and leave a hole in the center to insert the stem. Make eleven green bracts using 1/24 x 11¾ in. (1.5 x 300mm) strips and following steps 1 and 2.

15 Stick the bracts to the dome with tapered ends protruding from the rim. Let dry completely. Insert the stem through the hole in the dome and glue it at the bottom of the flower. Let dry completely, then fan out the bracts.

16 Glue the sepal in the center of the flower.

TIP If the dried petals are covered with a white residue from the glue, let them dry completely then use a clean, soft paintbrush to brush them with clean water and let dry again. This will remove the excess glue and make them clean and bright. Do not use too much water as this will make the paper very soggy and the petals will lose their shape.

Lotus Flower

The lotus flower is a symbol of purity and enlightenment in many Asian cultures. While rooted in the mud, its flowers blossom on the surface of the water, as if floating above worldly cares and desires. The color of the flower conveys different meanings—I chose pink (symbolic of the Buddha in Buddhism), but you can use blue (wisdom), purple (spirituality), red (love), white (purity), or gold (enlightenment).

Getting started

First cut all your strips using a steel ruler and paper cutter on a cutting mat (see Techniques page 120). The lotus flower has twenty-eight petals, made from 196 small O-shapes using 1⁄16 x 6 in. (2 x 150mm) strips, and twenty-eight large O-shapes using 1⁄16 x 11¾ in. (2 x 300mm) strips. The petals sit in an inverted dome and surround a stamen. The finished flower sits on a leaf.

- There are seven petals in the first (innermost) row. You will need seven 1⁄16 x 6 in. (2 x 150mm) and two 1⁄16 x 11¾ in. (2 x 300mm) pink paper strips for each one
- There are seven petals in the second row. You will need eleven 1⁄16 x 6 in. (2 x 150mm) and two 1⁄16 x 11¾ in. (2 x 300mm) pink paper strips for each one
- There are seven petals in the third row. You will need fifteen 1⁄16 x 6 in. (2 x 150mm) and two 1⁄16 x 11¾ in. (2 x 300mm) pink paper strips for each one
- There are seven petals in the fourth row. You will need nineteen 1⁄16 x 6 in. (2 x 150mm) and two 1⁄16 x 11¾ in. (2 x 300mm) pink paper strips for each one
- You will need fifteen ⅛ x 11¾ in. (5 x 300mm) and eighteen 1⁄16 x 11¾ in. (2 x 300mm) pink paper strips for the dome
- You will need two ¼ x 11¾ in. (7 x 300mm) yellow paper strips and one ¾ x 6 in. (20 x 150mm) yellow paper strip for the stamen
- You will need one A4 sheet of thick green paper for the leaf

You will need

Pink paper strips:
364 strips 1⁄16 x 6 in. (2 x 150mm)
64 strips 1⁄16 x 11¾ in. (2 x 300mm)
15 strips ⅛ x 11¾ in. (5 x 300mm)

Yellow paper strips:
2 strips ¼ x 11¾ in. (7 x 300mm)
1 strip ¾ x 6 in. (20 x 150mm)

Thick green paper:
1 A4-size sheet

Dark green poster paint

Steel ruler
Paper cutter
Cutting mat
Quilling comb
Needle tool
Glue
Quilling tool
Paintbrush
Mini Mold
Paper clip
Sharp pair of scissors
Toothpick
Dome shaper

Finished size

Approximately 4 in. (100mm) in diameter

Difficulty level

Moderate

Preparing the O-shapes

1 Make 196 small O-shapes, using strips measuring 1/16 x 6 in. (2 x 150mm) (See Techniques page 124). Wrap the strip around the comb until you reach the fourth and eleventh prongs. Make 28 large O-shapes, using strips measuring 1/16 x 11¾ in. (2 x 300mm). Wrap the strip around the comb until you reach the second and thirteenth prongs.

2 For each of the 28 petals, take one small O-shape, wrap it over a needle tool, and squeeze the sides to form a V-shape.

3 Apply glue along the inside edge with a needle tool (see Techniques page 119). Press the sides together to form a droplet.

4 Wrap the remaining small and large O-shapes around the body of a quilling tool, and press into a U-shape.

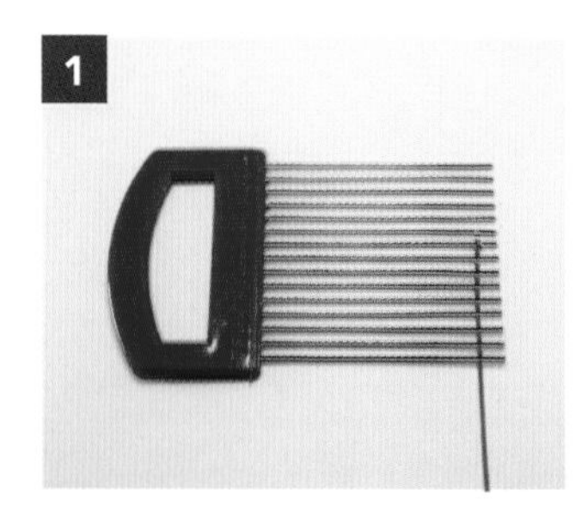

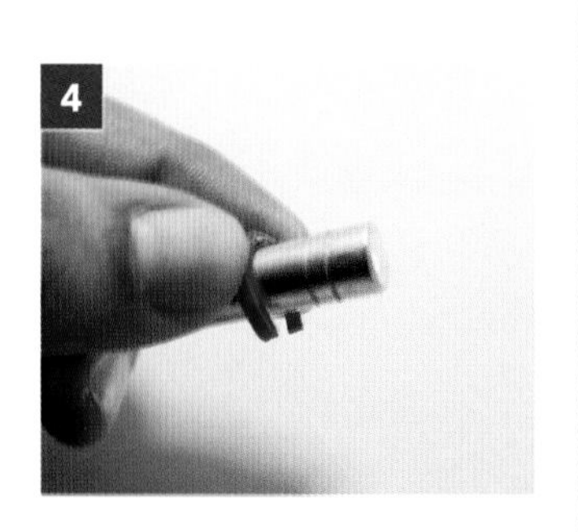

Making the petals

5 To make a petal, glue one small U-shape over a droplet. Wrap a 1/16 x 6 in. (2 x 150mm) strip around the edge, and glue in place.

6 Repeat step 5 to make the rest of the U-shapes required for the petals. Finish each of the first, second, third, and fourth row petals with one of the large U-shapes, and wrap it with one of the 1/16 x 11¾ in. (2 x 300mm) edging strips.

7 Apply glue to the reverse side of the petal with a brush, and leave it until almost dry, so that it holds its shape but remains malleable. Pinch the petal at both ends, then use a Mini Mold to shape it in the center to create a domed shape (see Techniques page 125).

8 Repeat steps 5 to 7 for all three sizes of petals, pressing those for the third and fourth rows into a deeper dome shape than those for the first and second rows.

Assembling the flower

9 To make a base to glue the petals to, quill a tight roll using the ⅛ x 11¾ in. (5 x 300mm) strips, and use a Mini Mold to press it into a dome shape approximately 1¼ in. (30mm) wide and ¾ in. (20mm) high.

10 Glue the first row of seven small petals onto the inside of the dome, and let dry.

11 Glue the second row of seven medium-sized petals onto the outside of the dome, alternating the position of the petals with those in the first row, and let dry. Glue the third row of seven large-sized petals in an alternating pattern, and let dry. Repeat for the fourth row, fanning the petals out a little.

12 Make another, smaller, dome to cover the base, using the 1/16 x 11¾ in. (2 x 300mm) strips. Glue in position and let dry.

Making the stamen

13 Take the ¼ x 11¾ in. (7 x 300mm) yellow strips, and cut a fine fringe along one edge with sharp scissors (see Techniques page 123). Take the ¾ x 6 in. (20 x 150mm) strip, and cut tapered triangles along one edge. Curl the triangles with an embossing tool and embossing pad (see Techniques page 124).

14 Tightly quill the two fringed strips together to form a roll, and glue in place. Glue the strip with tapered triangles around the roll. Glue the stamen in the center of the flower.

Making a leaf

15 Cut a leaf shape from green paper using the template on page 126. Paint the leaf shape with two coats of dark green poster paint. Let dry completely between coats.

16 Apply a third coat of paint, and before it dries, score the veins of the leaf with a toothpick. Let dry completely. Repeat steps 15 and 16 to make more leaves. Display your lotus flower on top of the leaves, as if it is floating on water.

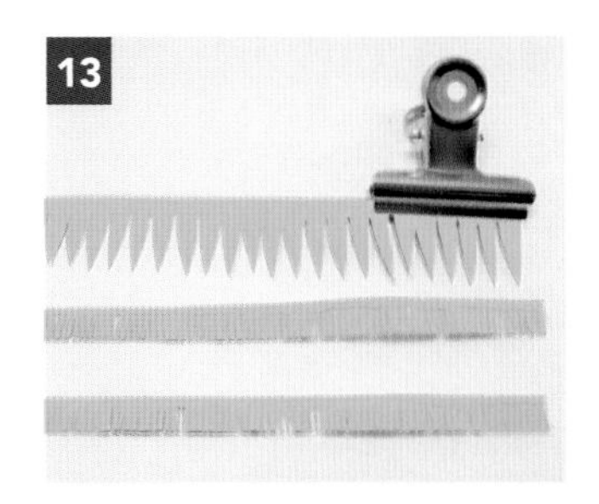

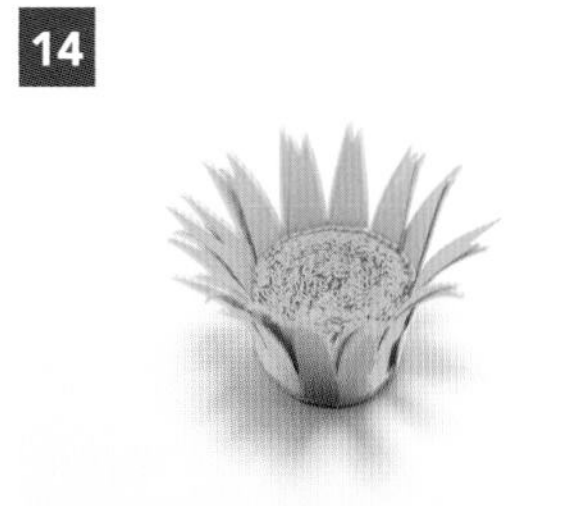

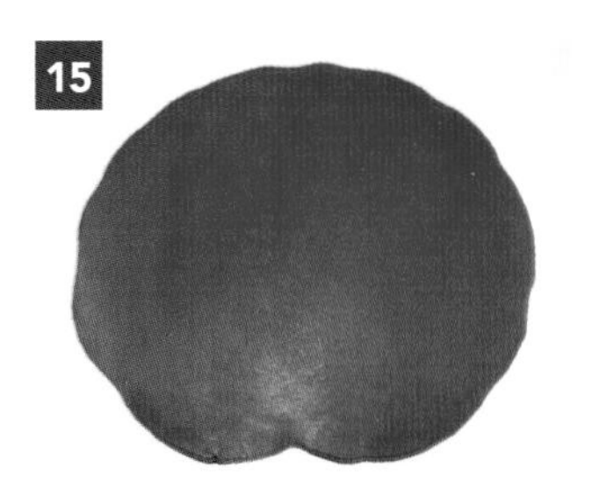

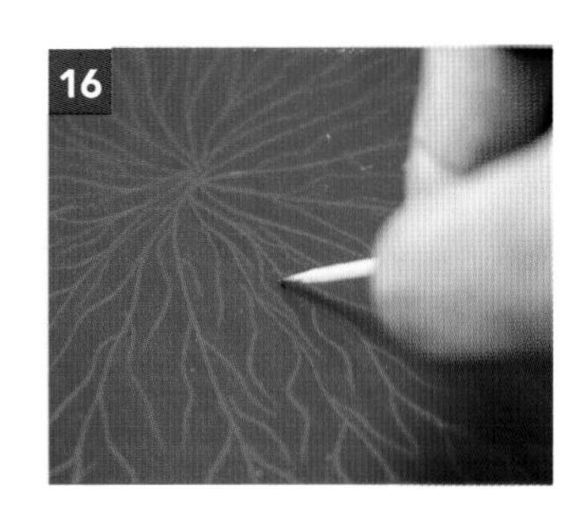

Poppy

The humble poppy has become symbolic of many things, from extravagance and beauty, to consolation for a loss in the family, and a way to remember the fallen in many wars and armed conflicts. This flower, with its tissue-like petals, is often seen growing by the roadside or at the edges of fields, where the seeds are left to flourish on their own—the triumph of nature over man.

Getting started

First cut all your strips using a steel ruler and paper cutter on a cutting mat (see Techniques page 120). The poppy flower has six petals in two sizes that are arranged around a stamen and supported by a stem.

- There are four long narrow petals. For each one you need nine 1/16 x 11¾ in. (2 x 300mm) red paper strips
- There are two short broad petals. For each one you need fourteen 1/16 x 11¾ in. (2 x 300mm) red paper strips
- For the sepal you will need three 1/16 x 11¾ in. (2 x 300mm) green paper strips; two 3/16 x 11¾ in. (4 x 300mm) fluorescent green paper strips; one ½ x 2 in. (12 x 50mm), one 1/16 x 11¾ in. (2 x 300mm), and four 1/32 x 7/16 in. (1 x 10mm) black paper strips

You will need

Red paper strips:
64 strips 1/16 x 11¾ in. (2 x 300mm)

Green paper strips:
3 strips 1/16 x 11¾ in. (2 x 300mm)

Fluorescent green paper strips:
2 strips 3/16 x 11¾ in. (4 x 300mm)

Black paper strips:
1 strip ½ x 2 in. (12 x 50mm)
1 strip 1/16 x 11¾ in. (2 x 300mm)
4 strips 1/32 x 7/16 in. (1 x 10mm)

Green paper-covered wire stem

Steel ruler
Paper cutter
Cutting mat
Pen
Paper
Cork board
Small-headed sharp pins
Quilling tool
Glue
Mini Mold
Needle tool
Paper clip
Sharp pair of scissors
Paintbrush

Finished size

Approximately 3 in. (76mm) in diameter

Difficulty level

Easy

Making the long, narrow petals

1 Using the template on page 126 draw the outline of a poppy petal 2 in. (50mm) wide and 2 in. (50mm) deep on a sheet of paper. Use small-headed sharp pins to attach it to a cork board at the corners. Quill a small roll at one end of a 1/16 x 11¾ in. (2 x 300mm) red strip. Pin the roll at the center of the bottom of the petal outline.

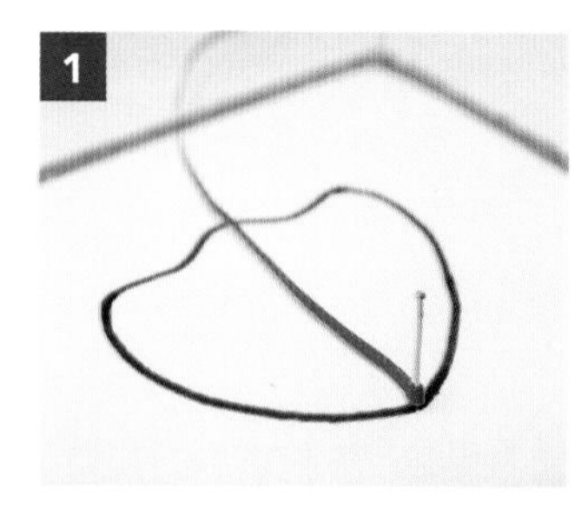

2 Insert a pin at the center of the top of the petal outline. This will be pin 1. Loop the strip around pin 1 from left to right. Pull the strip tight and glue it to the pinned roll.

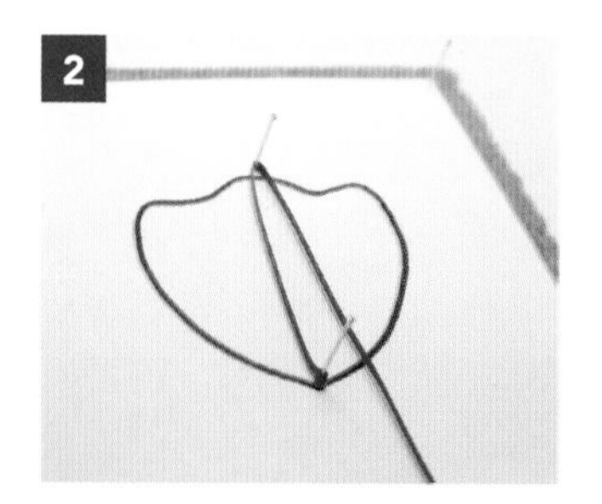

3 Place a second pin (pin 2) 1/16 in. (2mm) to the left of the pin 1. Loop the strip around pin 2, taking it from the left-hand side of the bottom pin, to the right-hand side of pin 2 and looping it around so that it is on the outside of the petal outline. Pull the strip tight and glue it to the pinned roll.

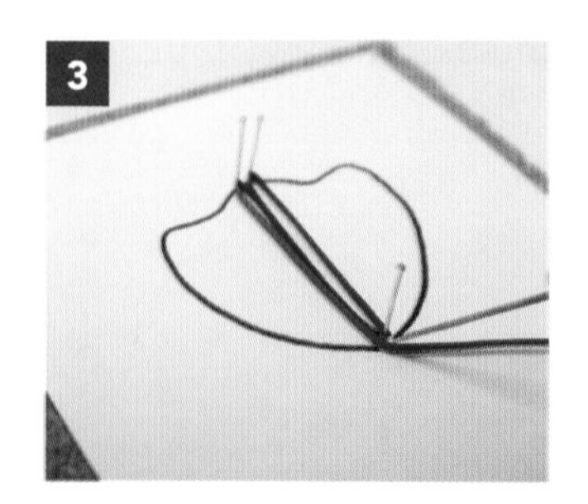

4 Place a pin (pin 3) 1/16 in. (2mm) to the right of pin 1. Loop the strip around pin 3, taking it from the right-hand side of the bottom pin, to the left-hand side of pin 3 and looping it around so that it is on the outside of the petal outline. Pull the strip tight and glue it to the pinned roll.

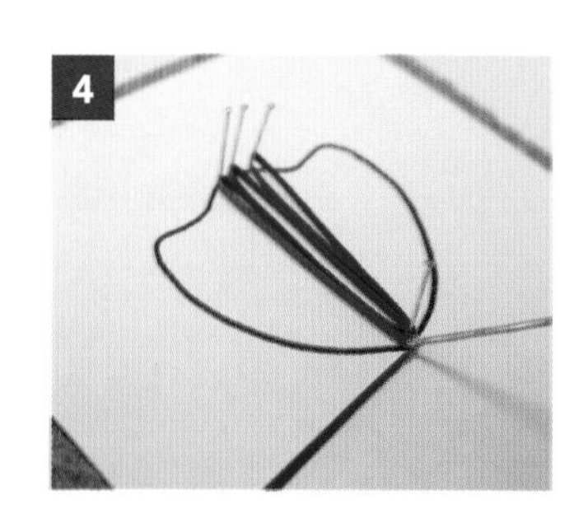

5 Repeat steps 3 and 4 by placing more pins along the top of the petal outline, one by one and alternating between the left and right sides. Glue the strip at the bottom and take care not to get glue on the sheet of paper or it will be difficult to remove the petal. Extend the strip as you work by joining a new strip to the end of the previous one (see Techniques, page 121).

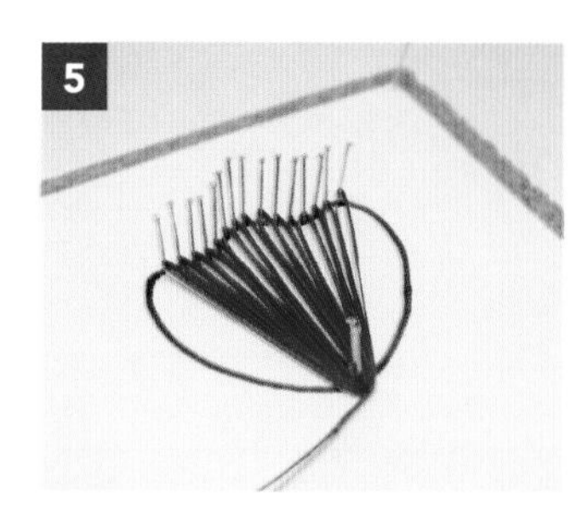

6 When the outline is full do not trim the end of the strip. Carefully apply glue to the outside of the tip of each loop of the paper strip. Attach the remaining paper strip to the glued points around the petal outline. Repeat this step then cut off the remaining paper strip.

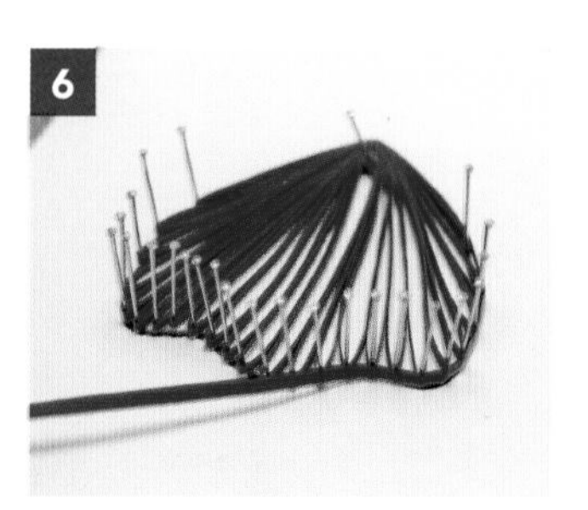

7 Remove the pin at the bottom of the petal and lift the petal off the paper. Slowly remove the petal from the pins. Leave the pins in place ready to make the rest of the petals. Repeat steps 2 to 7 to make four petals.

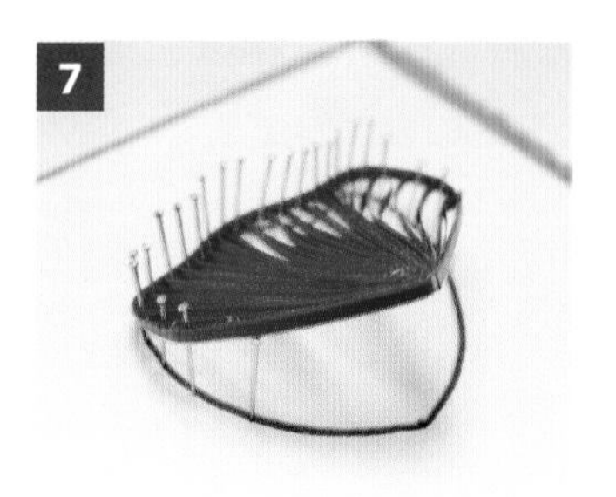

Making the short, broad petals

8 Using the template on page 126 draw the outline of a poppy petal 2¾ in. (70mm) wide and 1⅜ in. (30mm) deep on paper and attach it to a cork board as before. Make two petals following the instructions in steps 2 to 7.

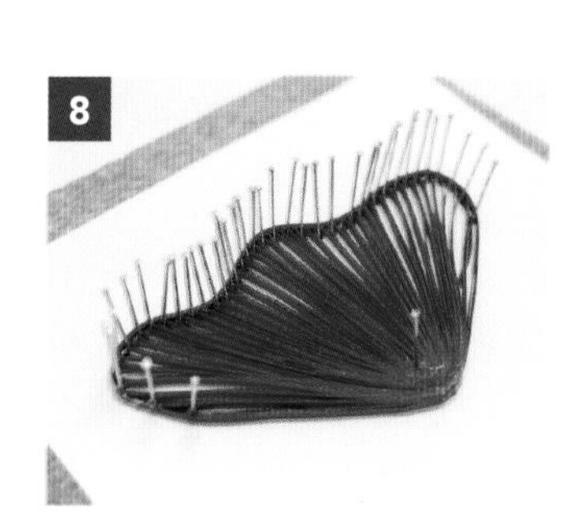

Making the sepal, pistil, and stamen

9 To make the sepal, quill three 1/16 x 11¾ in. (2 x 300mm) green strips and shape into a conical dome (see Techniques page 125). Glue from the inside.

10 To make the pistil, quill one fluorescent green 3/16 x 11¾ in. (4 x 300mm) strip and shape it in a dome. Repeat to make a second dome. Glue them together with one on top of the other.

11 To complete the pistil, glue four black strips 1/32 x 7/16 in. (1 x 10mm) so that they form a star shape on the top of the pistil.

12 To make the stamen, make a tight roll by quilling one black strip 1/16 x 11¾ in. (2 x 300mm). Fringe one black strip ½ x 2 in. (12 x 50mm) and glue it around the roll (see Techniques page 123).

13 Glue the pistil inside the stamen.

Assembling the flower

14 Glue the narrow petals to the inside of the sepal one at a time. Let dry completely.

15 Glue the broad petals inside the sepal.

16 Glue the pistil in the center of the flower.

TIP To make a stem for your poppy you will need a green taped wire stem. Follow the steps for assembling the chrysanthemum (see page 13) to make the sepal and assemble the flower and stem. You can manipulate the stem to make it wavy.

Sunflower

These flowers have been celebrated by artists including Vincent Van Gogh and Georgia O'Keefe, and are an emblem of long life, loyalty, and platonic love. They get their name from the fact that they are heliotropic—they slowly turn throughout the day so that they face the sun as it moves from east to west. Although they are renowned for growing very tall, others climb to just 6 inches (15cm) high.

Getting started

First cut all your strips using a steel ruler and paper cutter on a cutting mat. The sunflower has thirty petals of equal size. They are arranged around a stigma and supported by a sepal and four leaves

- There are thirty petals. For each one you need six 1/16 x 6 in. (2 x 150mm) yellow paper strips
- For the stigma you need two ¼ x 11¾ in. (7 x 300mm) black paper strips, one ¼ x 11¾ in. (7 x 300mm) light brown paper strip and twelve 13/32 x 11¾ in. (10 x 300mm) dark brown paper strips
- For the sepal and supporting ring you need two 1/16 x 11¾ in. (2 x 300mm) yellow paper strips and fifteen 1/16 x 11¾ in. (2 x 300mm) green paper strips
- For each leaf you need fifteen 1/16 x 11¾ in. (2 x 300mm) green paper strips

You will need

Yellow paper strips:
180 strips 1/16 x 6 in. (2 x 150mm)
2 strips 1/16 x 11¾ in. (2 x 300mm)

Black paper strips:
2 strips ¼ x 11¾ in. (7 x 300mm)

Light brown paper strip:
1 strip ¼ x 11¾ in. (7 x 300mm)

Dark brown paper strips:
12 strips 13/32 x 11¾ in. (10 x 300mm)

Green paper strips:
30 strips 1/16 x 11¾ in. (2 x 300mm)

Steel ruler
Paper cutter
Cutting mat
Quilling comb
Glue
Paintbrush
Paper clip
Paper cutting knife
Sharp pair of scissors
Quilling tool
Border Buddy
Mini Mold
Needle tool

Finished size

Approximately 3¾ in. (95mm) in diameter

Difficulty level

Moderate

Making the petals

1 For each petal, make five O-shapes using 1/16 x 6 in. (2 x 150mm) strips. (See Techniques page 124). Apply glue to the sides and glue them together in a row.

2 Pinch the open ends to seal and make a petal shape (see Techniques page 122). Wrap a 1/16 x 6 in. (2 x 150mm) strip around the petal to secure all five O-shapes in position. Repeat steps 1 and 2 to make thirty petals.

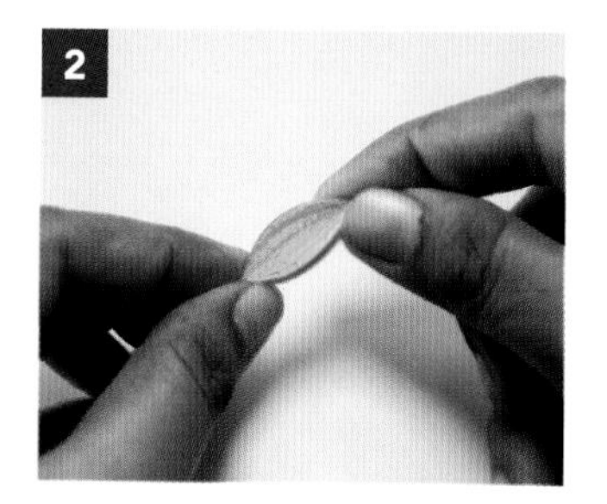

Shaping the petals

3 Use a soft paintbrush to apply glue to the back of one petal and let dry (see Techniques page 119).

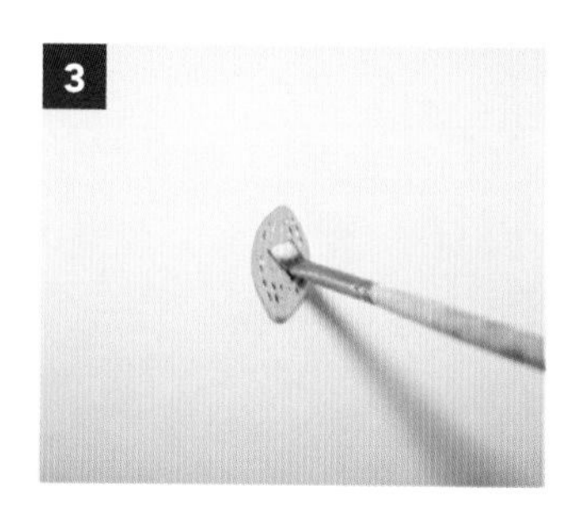

4 Shape the petal by pressing it around the handle of a thin paintbrush. Repeat with the remaining petals.

Making the stigma

5 Use a sharp pair of scissors to cut a fine fringe along one long edge of the black, light brown and dark brown paper strips (see Techniques page 123).

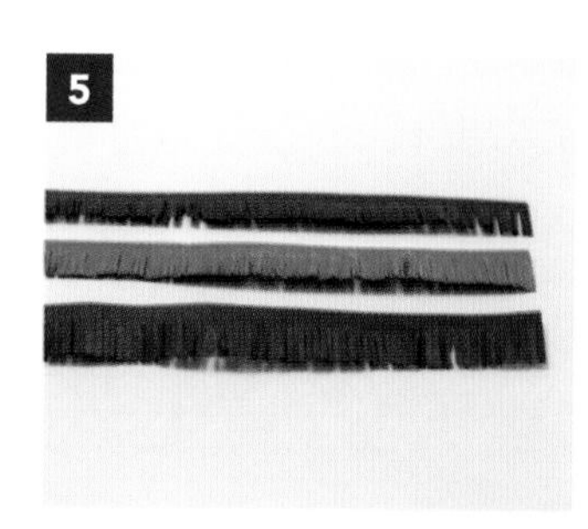

6 Use the strips to make a quilled roll (see Techniques page 121). Start with the two black strips, followed by one light brown and twelve dark brown strips. Glue the roll as you work to keep it in place.

TIP

If you want to display the sunflower and its leaf on a stem, insert one end of a thick green paper-covered wire stem (see page 21) into the center of the sepal and glue it in place. Glue the sepal to the back of the flower. Glue one end of a thin green paper-covered wire stem to the back of the leaf and wind the other end around the stem to secure it.

Assembling the petals

7 Make one $1\frac{7}{16}$ in. (35mm) ring using two $\frac{1}{16}$ x 11¾ in. (2 x 300mm) strips. Quill the strips around a circle-shaped Border Buddy or any circular base (see Techniques page 124).

8 Glue a row of fifteen petals around the ring and let dry completely.

9 Glue a second row of fifteen petals above the first so that they alternate with the first row. Press the bottom of the petals onto the ring so that they lift up to create a three-dimensional appearance. Let dry completely.

10 Place the stigma in the center of the flower and glue it from the back.

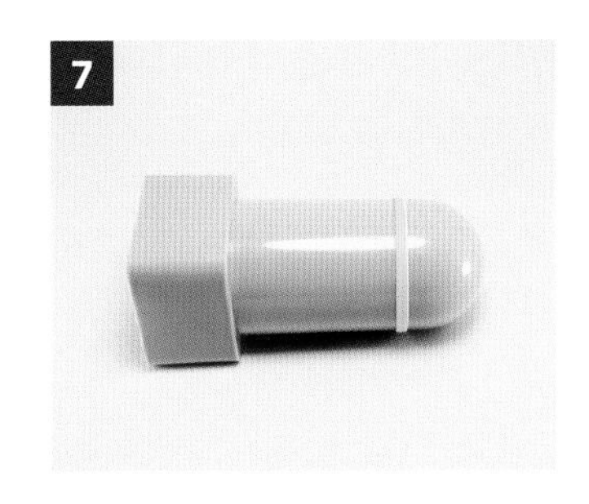

Making the sepal

11 Quill fifteen green strips $\frac{1}{16}$ x 11¾ in. (2 x 300mm) into a roll. Shape it in a shallow dome using a Mini Mold and secure with glue.

12 Attach the dome to the back of the flower.

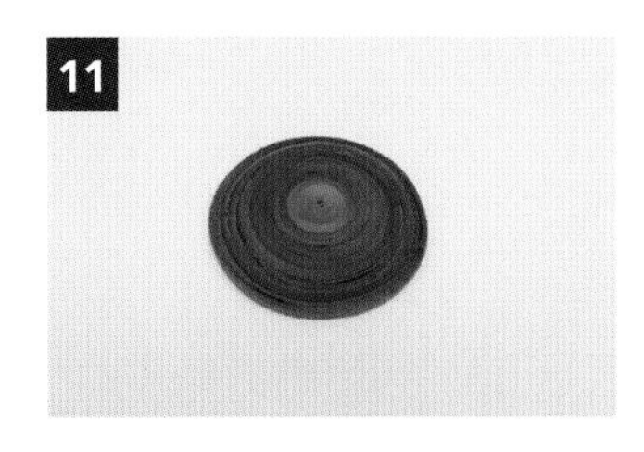

Making a leaf

13 Make fifteen O-shapes using fifteen green $\frac{1}{16}$ x 11¾ in. (2 x 300mm) strips. Take one O-shape; this will be the center shape. Glue a second O-shape to the left-hand side of the center O-shape and so that the tip is ⅛ in. (3mm) lower than the center one. Repeat on the right-hand side. Press the shapes at each end to seal.

14 Repeat step 12, making sure that the subsequent O-shapes are ⅛ in. (3mm) lower than the previous ones. Repeat until all the O-shapes have been used.

15 Apply glue to the back of the leaf and let dry.

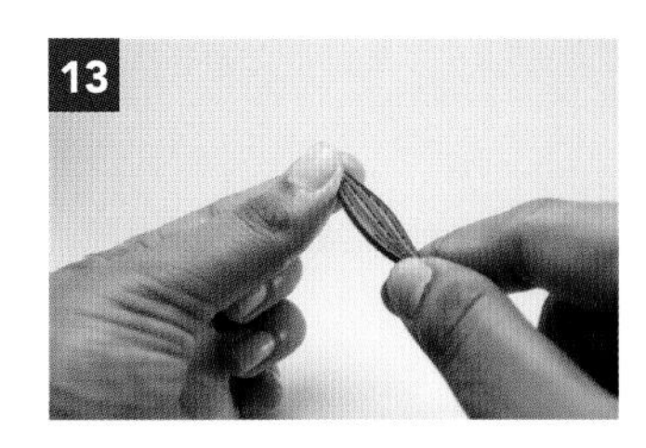

Fruits

They may look good enough to eat, but this strawberry, prickly pear, pineapple, and rambutan are made from quilled paper. Using vibrantly colored paper brings the fruit to life—and makes it look even more delicious.

Pineapple

A traditional expression of welcome and hospitality, the sweet flesh of the pineapple has been celebrated for centuries. It has been claimed that Christopher Columbus "discovered" it on his second trip to the Caribbean in 1493. On his return to Europe, he brought the pineapple plant which became a symbol of great riches—only the wealthy could possibly cultivate such an exotic fruit.

Getting started

First cut all your strips using a steel ruler and paper cutter on a cutting mat (see Techniques page 120). The pineapple is made from 80 berries arranged on an oval shape made from two domes that sits on a round base and is topped by a third dome and some leaves.

- For the larger dome for the oval you need thirty green strips 3⁄16 x 11¾ in. (5 x 300mm). For the smaller dome you need 30½ green strips 3⁄16 x 11¾ in. (5 x 300mm)

- For each of the sixty-four large berries you need one sea green strip ⅛ x 17¾ in. (3 x 450mm), one pale green strip ⅛ x 6 in. (3 x 150mm) and one cream strip ⅛ x 8⅝ in. (3 x 220mm)

- For each of the 16 small berries, each one requires one sea green strip ⅛ x 8⅝ in. (3 x 220mm), one pale green strip ⅛ x 6 in. (3 x 150mm) and one cream strip ⅛ x 8⅝ in. (3 x 220mm)

- For the base you need four ⅛ x 11¾ in. (3 x 300mm) pale green strips

- For the leaves you need a dome made from three ⅛ x 11¾ in. (3 x 300mm) dark green strips and two to three A4 sheets of green paper

You will need

Green paper strips:
60½ strips 3⁄16 x 11¾ in. (5 x 300mm)

Sea green paper strips:
64 strips ⅛ x 17¾ in. (3 x 450mm)
16 strips ⅛ x 8⅝ in. (3 x 220mm)

Pale green paper strips:
80 green strips ⅛ x 6 in. (3 x 150mm)
4 strips ⅛ x 11¾ in. (3 x 300mm)

Cream paper strips:
80 strips ⅛ x 8⅝ in. (3 x 220mm)

Dark green paper strips:
3 strips ⅛ x 11¾ in. (3 x 300mm)

Sheets of green paper:
2–3 A4-size sheets

Steel ruler
Paper cutter
Cutting mat
Mini Mold
Glue
Paintbrush
Quilling tool
Sharp pair of scissors
Needle tool

Finished size

Approximately 6¾ in. (170mm) high

Difficulty level

Moderate

Making of oval shape

1 Make two domes (see Techniques page 125). For the upper dome use thirty green strips 3/16 x 11¾ in. (5 x 300mm). For the bottom dome use thirty-and-a-half strips 3/16 x 11¾ in. (5 x 300mm). Use your fingers to gently push the domes to extend them until they are about 1 7/16 in. (35mm) tall. Glue them generously on the inside and let dry completely.

2 Glue the rims of the domes together to make an oval shape (see Techniques page 119). Let dry.

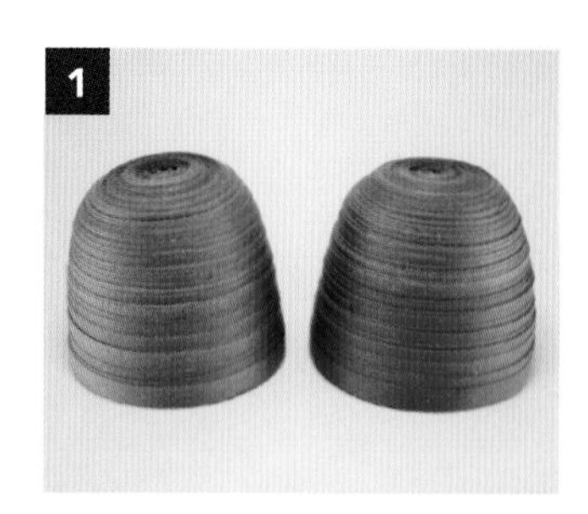

Making the berries

3 For each berry, take one cream strip. Find the point 3⅝ in. (90mm) from one end and join the pale green strip to it so that the strips overlap (see Techniques page 121). Find the point 5⅛ in. (130mm) from the joined end of the pale green strip, and join the dark green strip to it so that the strips overlap.

4 Starting with cream section, quill the joined strip into a roll (see Techniques page 121).

5 Loosen the roll slightly so that you can manipulate it but not so much that the coils start to separate. Press the loosened roll on five sides to create a pentagon.

6 Repeat steps 3 to 5 to make sixty-four large berries using sixty-four sea green strips ⅛ x 17¼ in. (3 x 450mm), sixty-four pale green strips ⅛ x 6 in. (3 x 150mm) and sixty-four cream strips ⅛ x 8⅝ in. (3 x 220mm). Make sixteen small berries using sixteen sea green strips ⅛ x 8⅝ in. (3 x 220mm), sixteen pale green strips ⅛ x 6 in. (3 x 150mm), and sixteen cream strips ⅛ x 8⅝ in. (3 x 220mm).

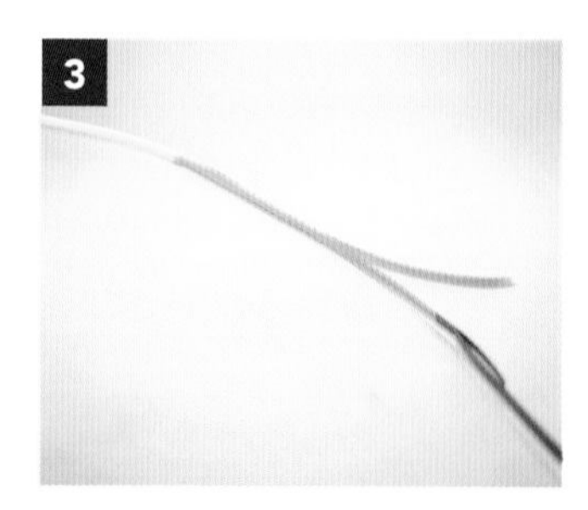

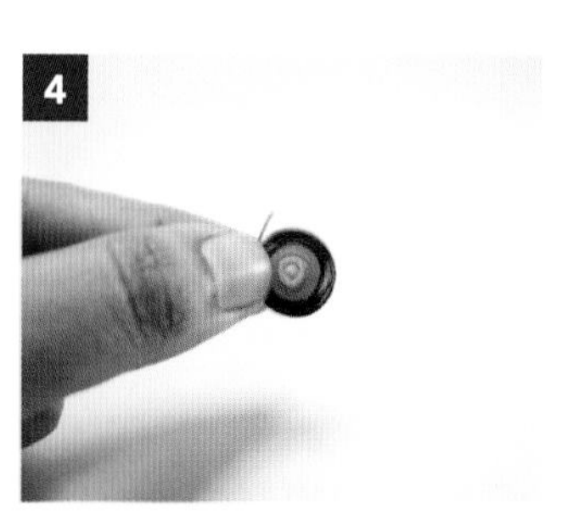

Making the pineapple

7 Glue the large berries around the oval, leaving a narrow border at the top and bottom (the large berries will be too big to fit here). Apply pressure to the berries so that they are tightly packed and there is no, or very little, space between them.

8 Attach a row of small berries around the top and bottom of the oval shape to fill the borders left in step 7.

9 Quill a roll using four pale green strips ⅛ x 11¾ in. (3 x 300mm). Shape it into a pentagon (see step 5).

10 Attach the roll at the bottom of the pineapple to make a base.

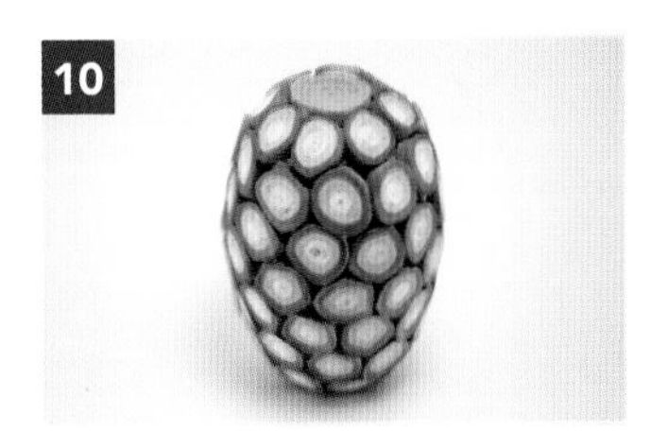

11 Quill a roll using three dark green paper strips ⅛ x 11¾ in. (3 x 300mm) and shape it into an elongated dome. Attach the dome to the top of the oval.

12 Using the templates on page 126 cut the leaves from the sheets of green paper (see Techniques page 123). Cut out five or six of each of the four sizes of leaf. Fold all the leaves in half lengthwise to create a line down the center.

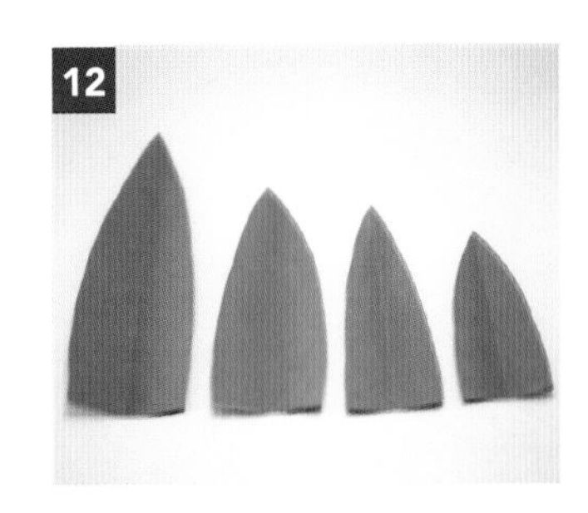

13 Starting with the longest leaves, glue them around the green dome one at a time.

14 Attach the second-longest leaves in front of the longest ones. Use progressively smaller leaves as you work outward.

15 Finally, attach the smallest leaves to the pineapple and let dry.

Strawberry

Every spring, the arrival of the first strawberries is a much-anticipated sign that summer is on its way. As a result, these soft fruits are said to symbolize rebirth, as well as friendship and righteousness. The red heart-shaped fruits are often associated with Venus, the Roman goddess of love.

You will need

Red paper strips:
30½ strips ⅛ x 11¾ in. (3 x 300mm)

Green paper strips (for leaves):
12 strips 1/32 x 10⅝in. (1 x 270mm)

Green paper strips (for stem):
1 strip ¼ x ¾ in. (6 x 20mm)

Green paper strips (for the small dome):
1 strip 1/32 x 7 in. (1 x 180mm)

Yellow paper:
1 A4-size sheet

Steel ruler
Paper cutter
Cutting mat
Quilling tool
Mini Mold
Glue
Paintbrush
Sharp pair of scissors
Needle tool

Finished size

Approximately 1 9/16 in. (40mm) high

Difficulty level

Easy

Getting started

First cut all your strips using a steel ruler and paper cutter on a cutting mat (see Techniques page 120). The strawberry is made from two domes covered with seeds and with a stem and leaves on the top.

- For the shallow dome you need fifteen-and-a-half ⅛ x 11¾ in. (3 x 300mm) red paper strips
- For the extended dome you need fifteen ⅛ x 11¾ in. (3 x 300mm) red paper strips
- For the stem and leaves you need one ¼ x ¾ in. (6 x 20mm) green paper strip, one 1/32 x 7 in. (1 x 180mm) green paper strip, and twelve 1/32 x 10½in. (1 x 270mm) green paper strips
- For the seeds you need one A4 sheet of yellow paper

Making the domes

1 Make two tight quilled rolls using fifteen strips ⅛ x 11¾ in. (3 x 300mm) for one and 15½ strips ⅛ x 11¾ in. (3 x 300mm) for the other (see Techniques page 121).

2 Shape the large roll into a perfect, shallow dome using a Mini Mold and set aside (see Techniques page 125). Shape the small roll into a dome using a Mini Mold, then use your fingers and thumb to slowly push the dome to extend it into a slightly conical dome as shown in the photograph. Glue the insides of the domes and let dry (see Techniques page 121).

3 When the shallow dome is almost dry but still malleable, invert it and press the center onto a Mini Mold to make a depression. Let dry completely.

1

2

3

Making the leaves and stem

4 Quill one green strip $\frac{1}{32}$ x $10\frac{5}{8}$in. (1 x 270mm) into a roll. Do not glue the end. Allow the roll to gradually loosen, holding it in place.

5 Hold the center of the coil, push it to one side then press the opposite side so that the leaf forms a teardrop shape (see Techniques page 122).

6 Repeat steps 4 and 5 to make twelve leaves. Glue the backs and let dry completely. Once they are dry, cut off the pointed end of all the leaves.

7 Quill a green paper strip $\frac{1}{32}$ x 7 in. (1 x 180mm) to make a small dome. Make a small stem by quilling a green paper strip ¼ x ¾ in. (6 x 20mm).

4

5

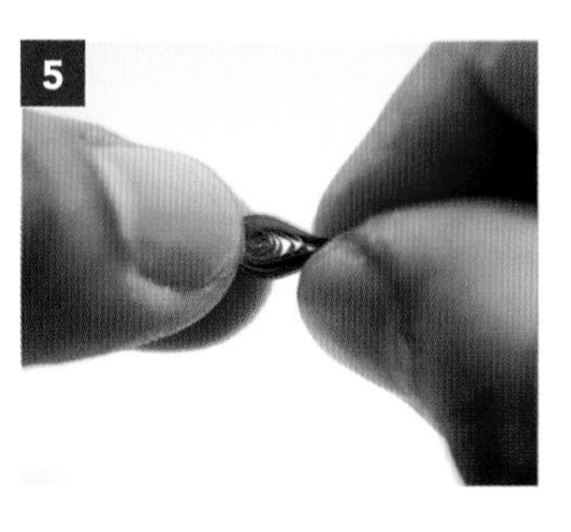

6

7

Assembling the strawberry

8 Apply glue to the inner rim of the shallow dome.

9 Attach the extended dome inside the shallow one to make a strawberry shape.

10 Glue the green dome in the center of the depression in the top of the strawberry. Then glue the stem in the center of the green dome.

11 Glue the leaves around the edge of the green dome one at a time with the cut ends at the bottom.

12 Cut small teardrops from the yellow sheet of paper until you have enough to decorate the surface of the strawberry.

13 Glue the teardrops onto the strawberry in an alternating pattern to create the seeds. Let dry.

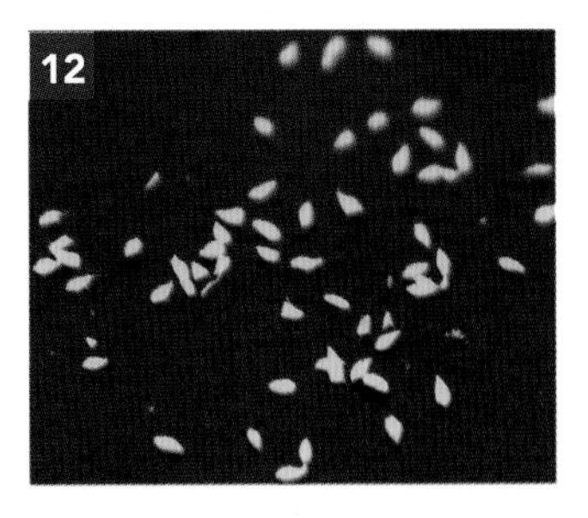

Prickly Pear

A member of the cactus family, the prickly pear has flat, fleshy, green-colored pads that look like large leaves. The pads, which grow quickly and at odd angles, store moisture and are edible. Although it can tolerate a wide range of temperatures, the prickly pear grows best in desert-like conditions and can be found in the United States, Mexico, South America, Africa, Australia, and the Mediterranean.

Getting started

First cut all your strips using a steel ruler and paper cutter on a cutting mat (see Techniques page 120). The cactus has seven sections, seven fruits, and thirty thorns. It sits in a pot.

- For the first section you need seven ⅛ x 11¾ in. (3 x 300mm) green strips; for the second section you need six ⅛ x 11¾ in. (3 x 300mm) green strips; for the third and fourth sections you need five ⅛ x 11¾ in. (3 x 300mm) green strips each; for the fifth section you need four ⅛ x 11¾ in. (3 x 300mm) green strips; and for the sixth and seventh sections you need two ⅛ x 11¾ in. (3 x 300mm) green strips each
- For each fruit you need one 1⁄32 x 2 in. (1 x 50mm) and one 1⁄32 x 1 3⁄16 in. (1 x 30mm) dark pink strip, and one 1⁄32 x 1 in. (1 x 25mm) cream strip
- For each thorn you need one 1⁄32 x ¾ in. (1 x 20mm) dark brown strip and spikes cut from two 13⁄32 x 2 19⁄32 in. (10 x 60mm) and two 3⁄16 x 2 19⁄32 in. (5 x 60mm) white paper strips
- For the pot you need ten ⅛ x 11¾ in. (3 x 300mm) brown paper strips and an A4 sheet of brown paper

You will need

Green paper strips:
31 strips ⅛ x 11¾ in. (3 x 300mm)

Dark pink paper strips:
7 strips 1⁄32 x 2 in. (1 x 50mm)
7 strips 1⁄32 x 1 3⁄16 in. (1 x 30mm)

Cream paper strips:
7 strips 1⁄32 x 1 in. (1 x 25mm)

Dark brown paper strips:
30 strips 1⁄32 x ¾ in. (1 x 20mm)

White paper strips:
2 strips 13⁄32 x 2 19⁄32 in. (10 x 60mm)
2 strips 3⁄16 x 2 19⁄32 in. (5 x 60mm)

Brown paper strips:
10 strips ⅛ x 11¾ in. (3 x 300mm)

Brown paper:
1 A4-size sheet

Steel ruler
Paper cutter
Cutting mat
Quilling tool
Glue
Needle tool
Mini Mold
Sharp pair of scissors

Finished size

Approximately 5 in. (125mm) high

Difficulty level

Moderate

Making the cactus

1 Quill seven ⅛ x 11¾ in. (3 x 300mm) green strips to make a segment of the stem (see Techniques page 121). Loosen the roll a little.

2 Press the loosened roll from the bottom to shape it into a teardrop shape (see Techniques page 122). Glue in place (see Techniques page 119). Glue the back of the shape and let dry. This will be the bottom (largest) segment of the cactus plant.

3 Repeat steps 1 and 2 to make six more segments, one using six ⅛ x 11¾ in. (3 x 300mm) green strips; two using five ⅛ x 11¾ in. (3 x 300mm) green strips; one using four ⅛ x 11¾ in. (3 x 300mm) green strips; and two using two ⅛ x 11¾ in. (3 x 300mm) green strips. Shape and arrange the seven segments as shown in the photograph.

Making the prickly pear fruit

4 Quill one 1/32 x 2 in. (1 x 50mm) dark pink paper strip into a tapering dome on the quilling tool as shown in the photograph. You can also make a roll and give it a tapering shape by manipulating it with a needle tool. Glue from the inside and let dry.

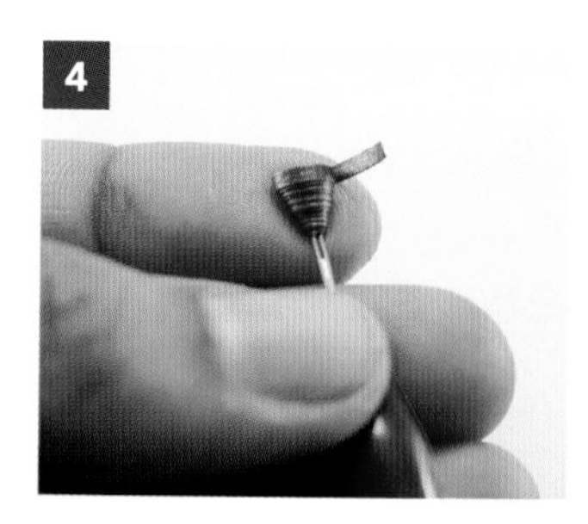

5 Join one 1/32 x 1 in. (1 x 25mm) cream paper strip and one 1/32 x 1 3/16 in. (1 x 30mm) dark pink paper strip and quill into a roll, starting at the cream end.

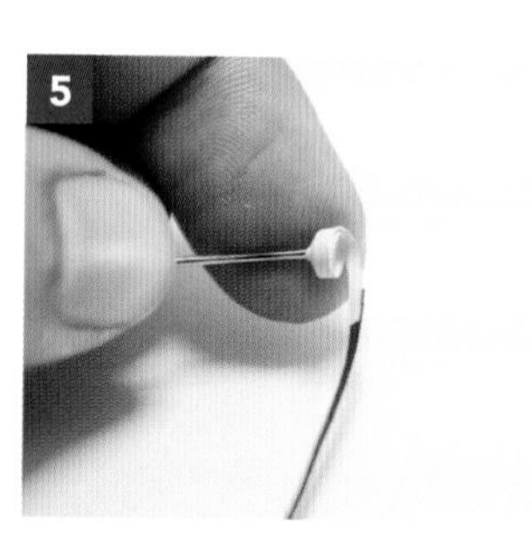

6 Shape the quilled strip on a Mini Mold (see Techniques page 125).

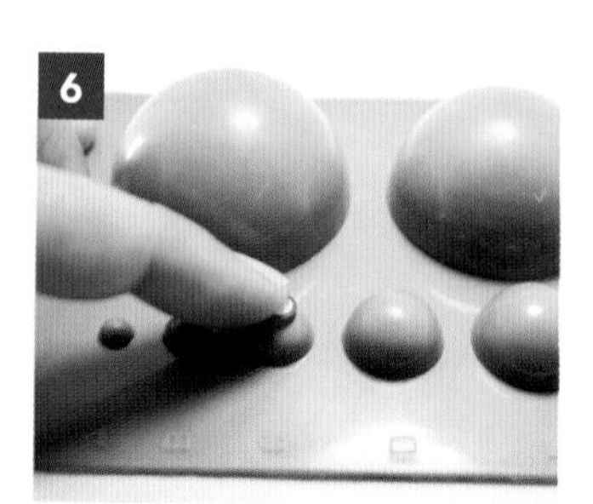

7 Glue the quilled roll to the top of the tapering dome to make the prickly pear fruit. Repeat steps 4 to 7 to make a total of seven fruits.

Assembling the cactus

8 Assemble the cactus stem segments and glue them together as shown in the photograph, or as desired.

9 Roll one 1/32 x ¾ in. (1 x 20mm) dark brown strip into a roll. Repeat to make a total of 30 small rolls.

10 Glue the small rolls to the stem segments, distributing them proportionately on each segment.

11 To make the thorns, glue the two 13/32 x 2 19/32 in. (10 x 60mm) and the two 3/16 x 2 19/32 in. (5 x 60mm) strips of white paper together to make hard strips. Cut thin triangles from both strips, as shown in the photograph.

12 Glue a small thorn onto each brown roll, followed by a large thorn. Let dry.

13 Glue the prickly pear fruits on top of the stem segments as shown in the photograph.

Making the pot

14 Quill ten ⅛ x 11¾ in. (3 x 300mm) brown paper strips into a roll. Use your fingers to shape it into a tapering dome. Flatten the base. Glue the inside of the dome and let dry.

15 Cut a 1-in. (25mm) diameter disk from the sheet of brown paper. Cut a rectangle about 1/16 x ¾ in. (2 x 20mm) from the center. Glue inside the pot and let dry.

16 Glue the base of the prickly pear cactus inside the rectangle.

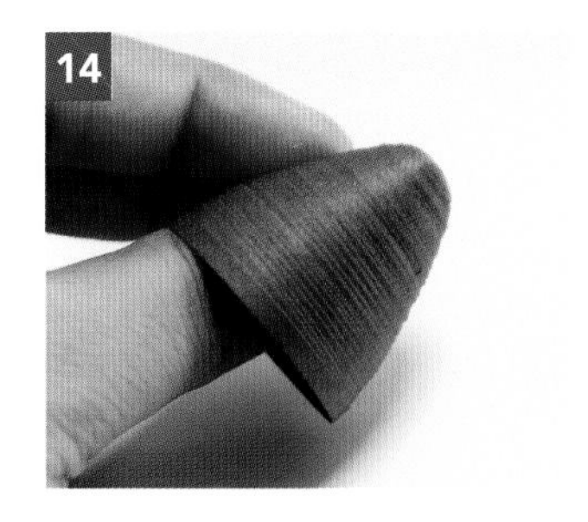

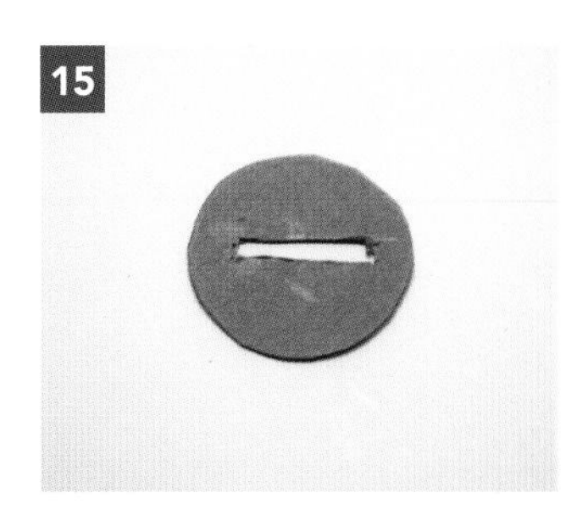

Rambutan

The rambutan gets its name from the hairs that cover its surface. These fleshy, pliable spikes are not sharp, and can be removed with the red rind. It is a member of the lychee family, and the rambutan's edible white flesh sits under the rind. The fruits grow in clusters on evergreen trees and are common in tropical countries such as Thailand, Malaysia, India, Indonesia, the Philippines, and Australia.

Getting started

First cut all your strips using a steel ruler and paper cutter on a cutting mat (see Techniques page 120). The rambutan is made from two domes which are joined together and decorated with hairs.

- For the larger dome you need fifteen-and-a-half 3/16 x 11¾ in. (5 x 300mm) red paper strips
- For the smaller dome you need fifteen 3/16 x 11¾ in. (5 x 300mm) red paper strips
- For the hairs you need two ¼ x 7¾ in. (7 x 200mm) green paper strips

You will need

Red paper strips:
30½ strips 3/16 x 11¾ in. (5 x 300mm)

Green paper strips:
2 strips ¼ x 7¾ in. (7 x 200mm)

Steel ruler
Paper cutter
Cutting mat
Quilling tool
Mini Mold
Glue
Paintbrush
Sharp pair of scissors
Needle tool

Finished size

Approximately 2½ in. (65mm) long

Difficulty level

Easy

Making the domes

1 Make two tight quilled rolls (see Techniques page 121); use fifteen 3⁄16 x 11¾ in. (5 x 300mm) red strips for one dome and fifteen-and-a-half 3⁄16 x 11¾ in. (5 x 300mm) red strips for the other.

2 Mold both rolls into a perfect dome using a Mini Mold (see Techniques page 125). Then use your fingers and thumb to shape each roll, slowly pushing the domes to elongate them.

3 The finished domes should be elongated as shown in the photograph.

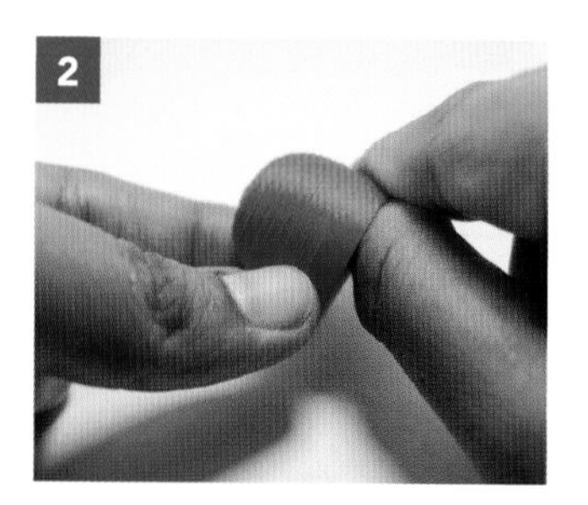

4 Glue the inside of both domes (see Techniques page 119). Let dry.

5 Apply glue to the inner rim of the larger dome. Position the smaller dome inside the larger dome to create an oval shape.

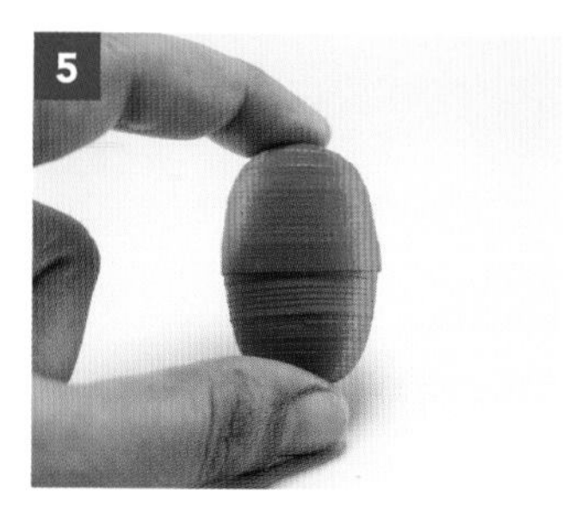

Making the hairs

6 Glue one ¼ x 7¾ in. (7 x 200mm) green strip onto the second ¼ x 7¾ in. (7 x 200mm) green strip to reinforce them. Let dry.

7 Use a sharp pair of scissors to cut thin spikes from the reinforced paper strip, as shown in the photograph.

8 Cut as many spikes as needed to decorate the surface of the fruit.

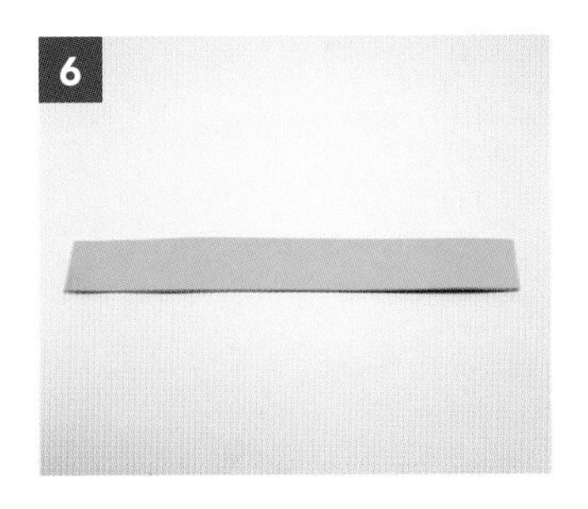

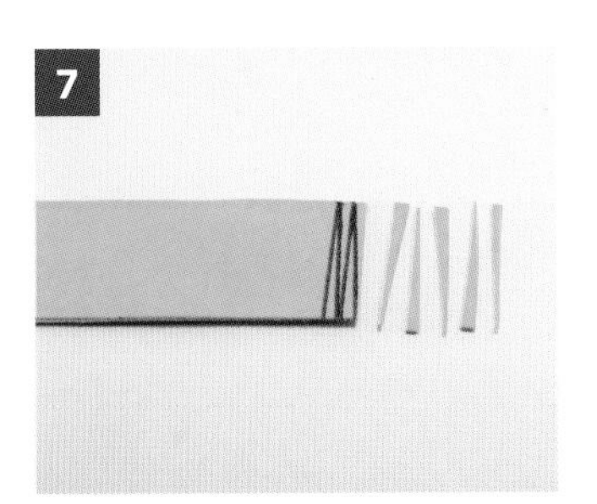

Assembling the fruit

9 Starting at the top of the fruit, glue the spikes in place with the help of a needle tool.

10 Continue to glue the hairs in place, leaving appropriate gaps between them.

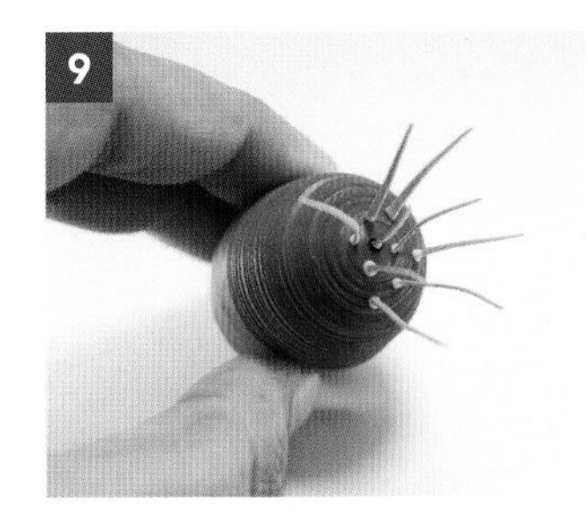

Insects

Capture the beauty of some of the world's smallest creatures using quilled paper O-shapes and rolls. Here a beetle, dragonfly, butterfly, and bee are brought to life in intricate detail, from the translucent wings of the dragonfly to the pollen sacs on the bee's legs.

Beetle

There are more than 360,000 species of beetle and they come in many sizes: The rhinoceros beetle can grow up to 8 inches (20cm) long, while one of the smallest, the featherwing beetle, can be the size of a grain of sand. For the ancient Egyptians, scarab beetles were associated with the god Khepri, a god of creation, the movement of the sun, and rebirth. Khepri was believed to roll the morning sun over the horizon at daybreak.

Getting started

First cut all your strips using a steel ruler and paper cutter on a cutting mat (see Techniques page 120). The beetle has an abdomen, thorax, and head; six legs; two wings, and two antennae.

- For the abdomen you need six ⅛ x 11¾ in. (3 x 300mm) black paper strips
- For the thorax you need four ⅛ x 11¾ in. (3 x 300mm) black paper strips
- For the head you need one ⅛ x 11¾ in. (3 x 300mm) black paper strip
- For each of the six legs you need one 1⁄32 x 1 3⁄16 in. (1 x 30mm) and one 1⁄32 x 5⁄16 in. (1 x 8mm) hard black paper strip
- For the wings you need three 1⁄24 x 11¾ in. (1.5 x 300mm) green paper strips
- For the antennae you need one 1⁄32 x 11⁄16 in. (1 x 17mm) hard black paper strip

You will need

Black paper strips:
11 strips ⅛ x 11¾ in. (3 x 300mm)

Hard black paper strips:
6 strips 1⁄32 x 1 3⁄16 in. (1 x 30mm)
6 strips 1⁄32 x 5⁄16 in. (1 x 8mm)
1 strip 1⁄32 x 11⁄16 in. (1 x 17mm)

Green paper strips:
3 strips 1⁄24 x 11¾ in. (1.5 x 300mm)

Black and white paper:
1 (1 in./25mm) square of each

Steel ruler
Paper cutter
Cutting mat
Quilling tool
Mini Mold
Glue
Paintbrush
Needle tool
Paper knife
Sharp pair of scissors

Finished size

Approximately 2¼ in. (55mm) long

Difficulty level

Easy

Making the body

1 Make a roll using six ⅛ x 11¾ in. (3 x 300mm) black strips (see Techniques page 121). Shape it into a dome using a Mini Mold (see Techniques page 125) and glue it from the inside. When it is completely dry, press it from two points to get a flat side as shown in the photograph.

2 Now press the center of the flat side toward the interior of the dome to make a curve. This is the abdomen.

3 Make another dome using four ⅛ x 11¾ in. (3 x 300mm) black strips. Glue and let dry. Press the dome from two points to get a flat side in the same way as the previous dome.

4 Press the flat side from the center toward the outer side of the dome. This is the thorax (center) section.

5 Glue the flat side of the thorax to the flat side of the abdomen and let dry.

6 To make the head, make a roll using one ⅛ x 11¾ in. (3 x 300mm) black strip. Press it from two points to get a flat side as before.

7 Use a needle tool to press an indentation into the center of the side of the dome opposite the flat side to make the head.

8 Glue the flat side of the head onto the front of the thorax.

Making the wings

9 Make a roll using one-and-a-half 1/24 x 11¾ in. (1.5 x 300mm) green strips. Slightly loosen the roll, keeping the coils even. Do not loosen it too much or the gaps between the coils will be too big. Glue the open end to secure it in place.

10 Press the loosened roll into a leaf shape (see Techniques page 122). Then press as shown in the photograph to give it the shape of a wing. Repeat steps 9 and 10 to make a second wing. Glue the backs of the wings and let dry.

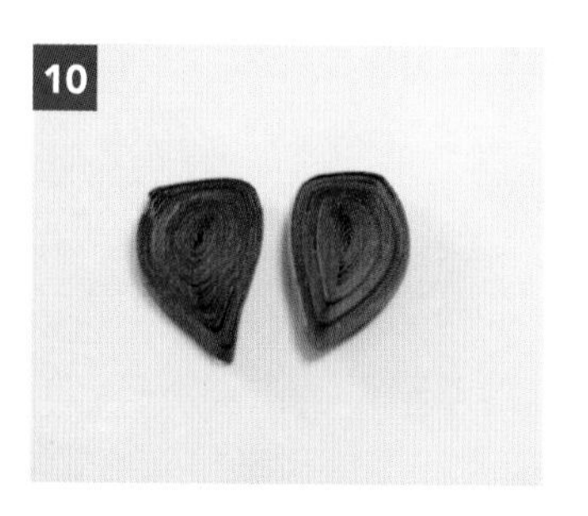

Making the antennae

11 Twist one 1/32 x 11/16 in. (1 x 17mm) hard black strip between your fingers to make a tight coil.

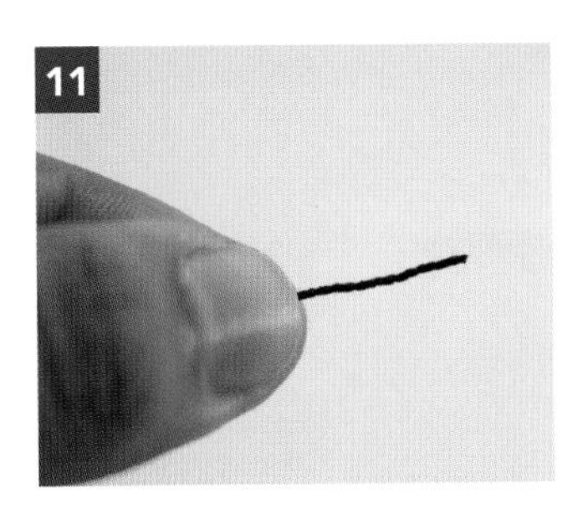

12 Fold the strip in half. Now curl each end as shown in the photograph. The curls should stay in place. Set aside.

Making the eyes

13 Use a paper knife to cut two small disks from the sheet of black paper. Glue them to the white sheet. Cut out the black circles with a border of white paper to create the eyes.

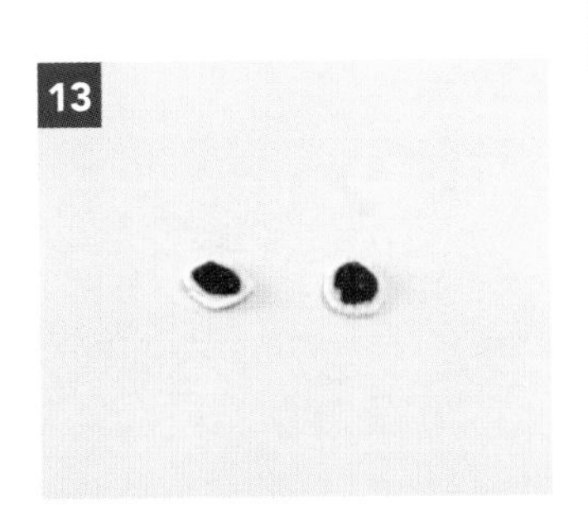

Making the legs

14 Fold one hard black strip 1/32 x 1 3/16 in. (1 x 30mm) at the points 3/8 in. (8mm) and 3/4 in. (16mm) from one end. Glue the two short sections together and let dry. Glue the short sections to the long section and let dry.

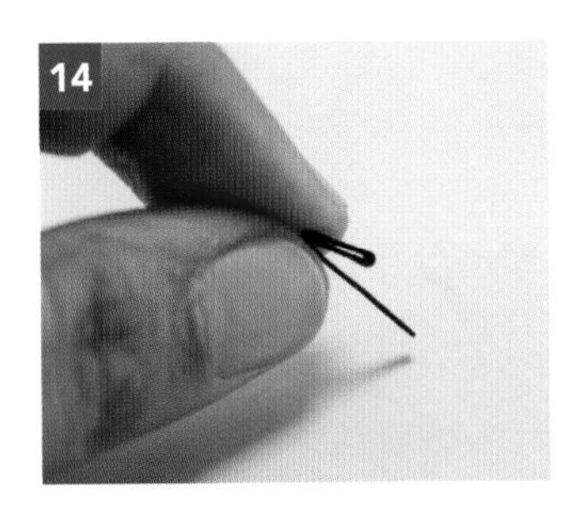

15 Take a hard black paper 1/32 x 5/16 in. (1 x 8mm) strip and glue it to the unfolded end of the first strip 1/4 in. (6mm) from one end. Fold the remaining 1/16 in. (2mm) of the strip to create an arc as shown in the photograph. Repeat to make six legs.

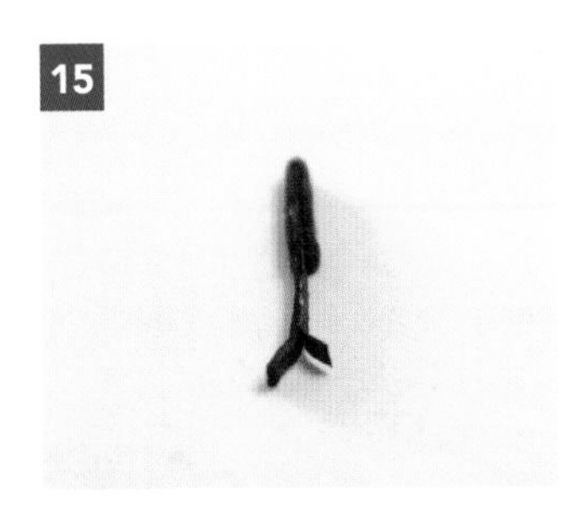

Assembling the beetle

16 Glue the wings to the abdomen; the antennae to the front of the head; the legs to the sides of the body; and the eyes to the head as shown in the photograph. Let dry.

Butterfly

The metamorphosis of a caterpillar into a butterfly has inspired many cultures to see these insects as symbolic of transformation and resurrection. They pollinate plants and provide food (especially in their caterpillar stage) for birds, mammals, and other insects. There are more than 20,000 species of butterfly, which means there's plenty of inspiration if you want to create your own butterfly design.

Getting started

First cut all your strips using a steel ruler and paper cutter on a cutting mat (see Techniques page 120). The butterfly has two wings, one body, and two antennae.

- For the wings you need forty-three-and-a-half ⅛ x 17¾ in. (3 x 450mm) yellow strips; four ⅛ x 17¾ in. (3 x 450mm), twenty-two ⅛ x 8⅞ in. (3 x 225mm), ten ⅛ x 4⅜ in. (3 x 112mm), and sixty-two ⅛ x 2¼ in. (3 x 56mm) black strips; and sixty-two ⅛ x 2¼ in. (3 x 56mm) white strips
- For the body and antennae you need one A4 sheet of black paper and one 1⁄32 x 1 9⁄16 in. (1 x 40mm) black strip

You will need

Yellow paper strips:
43½ strips ⅛ x 17¾ in. (3 x 450mm)

Black paper strips:
4 strips ⅛ x 17¾ in. (3 x 450mm)
22 strips ⅛ x 8⅞ in. (3 x 225mm)
10 strips ⅛ x 4⅜ in. (3 x 112mm)
62 strips ⅛ x 2¼in. (3 x 56mm)
1 strip 1⁄32 x 1 9⁄16 in. (1 x 40mm)

White paper strips:
62 strips ⅛ x 2¼in. (3 x 56mm)

Black paper:
1 A4-size sheet

Steel ruler
Paper cutter
Cutting mat
Quilling tool
Glue
Paintbrush
Needle tool
Sharp pair of scissors

Finished size

Approximately 4 in. (100mm) wide

Difficulty level

Moderate

Making the wings

1 Using the template on page 127 draw or photocopy the right side of the butterfly onto a sheet of paper.

2 Here, the different sections of the design are represented by differently colored dots.

3 To make each of the sections marked with white dots, quill a roll using the ⅛ x 17¾ in. (3 x 450mm) yellow strips joined with a ⅛ x 8⅞ in. (3 x 225mm) black strip (see Techniques page 121).

4 Place the roll on the appropriate section of the design, then loosen it so that, when pressed, the roll takes the shape and size of the section.

5 Press the roll until it is the desired size, then glue the free end of the strip to the roll (see Techniques page 119).

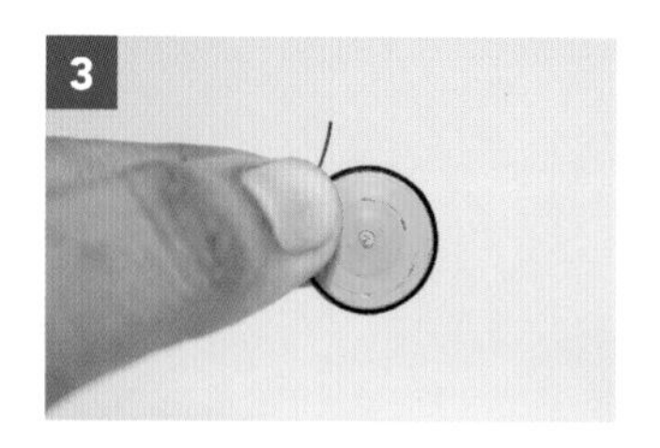

6 Press the roll tightly into shape using your fingers and pressing from all sides as required.

7 Repeat steps 3 to 6 to make the second section marked with a white dot.

8 To make the section marked by the pink dot, quill a roll using two ⅛ x 17¾ in. (3 x 450mm) yellow strips joined with a ⅛ x 8⅝ in. (3 x 225mm) black strip.

9 As this section is long and narrow in shape, loosen the roll more than the earlier ones to get the desired shape and size.

10 Press the roll into a narrow, elongated shape.

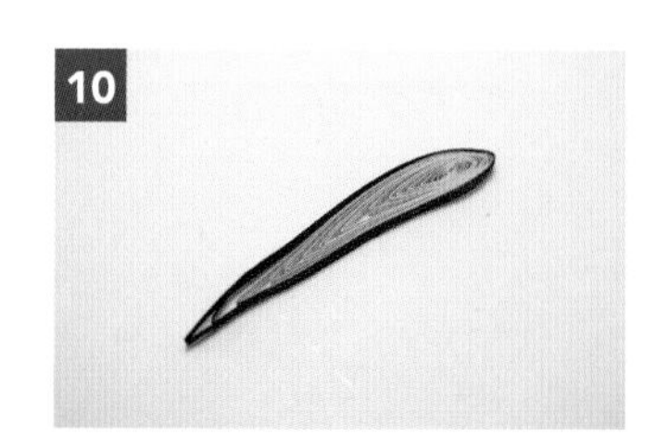

11 Make the remaining sections of the upper wing as follows, referring to step 2 to identify the sections:

For the section marked with a purple dot use one-and-a-half ⅛ x 17¾ in. (3 x 450mm) yellow strips joined with one ⅛ x 8⅞ in. (3 x 225mm) black strip.

For the section marked with a blue dot use one-and-a-half ⅛ x 17¾ in. (3 x 450mm) yellow strips joined with one ⅛ x 8⅞ in. (3 x 225mm) black strip.

For the section marked with a green dot use one ⅛ x 17¾ in. (3 x 450mm) yellow strip joined with one ⅛ x 8⅞ in. (3 x 225mm) black strip.

For the section marked with an orange dot use half a ⅛ x 17¾ in. (3 x 450mm) yellow strip joined with one ⅛ x 4⅜ in. (3 x 112mm) black strip.

12 Take one ⅛ x 17¾ in. (3 x 450mm) black strip. Mark a point on the strip equal to the length of the quilled section made for the bottom of the wing.

13 Fold the strip at the marked point, then fold whole strip in an equal zigzag to make a thick base. Glue each fold together so they stick firmly.

11

12

13

14 Glue this thick base to the section which is at the bottom of the wing.

15 Now start gluing all the sections together along the sides only. Do not glue them to the bottom.

16 Attach all the sections, following the design in step 2, remembering that the quilled sections may vary when compared to the drawn ones. Also, as the rolls are not glued at the bottom, they cannot be tightly packed and so the wings might look bigger. To gauge the actual size, press the wing from the top and bottom to see if it fits the shape on the paper.

17 Make a second upper wing section following steps 1 to 16. Flip over the wing used in step 2 so it is a mirror image of the first wing.

18 Use a paintbrush to apply a layer of glue to the back of the wings.

14

15

16

17

18

19 As the glue starts to dry, use your fingers to press the wings and tightly pack the coils together.

20 Repeat steps 3 to 10 to make the lower section of the wing as follows:

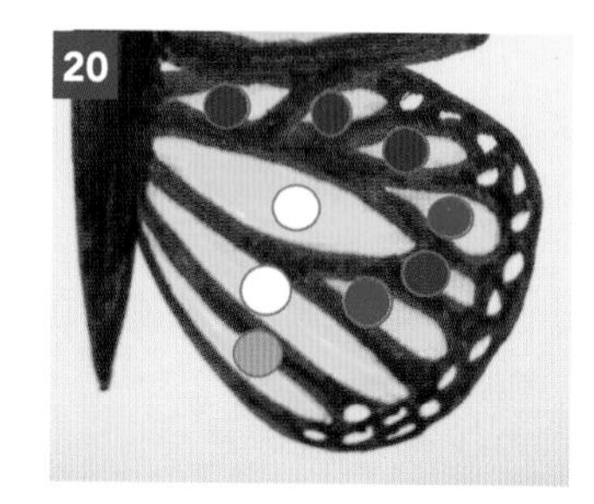

For each of the sections marked with white dots, use two ⅛ x 17¾ in. (3 x 450mm) yellow strips joined with one ⅛ x 8⅞ in. (3 x 225mm) black strip.

For each of the sections marked with green dots, use one ⅛ x 17¾ in. (3 x 450mm) yellow strip joined with one ⅛ x 8⅝ in. (3 x 225mm) black strip.

For the section marked with an orange dot, use one-and-a-half ⅛ x 17¾ in. (3 x 450mm) yellow strips joined with one ⅛ x 8⅝ in. (3 x 225mm) black strip.

For each of the sections marked with blue dots, use half of one ⅛ x 17¾ in. (3 x 450mm) yellow strip joined with one ⅛ x 4⅜ in. (3 x 112mm) black strip.

For the section marked with a maroon dot, use one-quarter of one ⅛ x 17¾ in. (3 x 450mm) yellow strip joined with one ⅛ x 4⅜ in. (3 x 112mm) black strip.

21 Make all the sections for the lower wing using the same techniques as for the upper wings. Join the sections together. Repeat to complete the second wing.

22 Repeat steps 11 and 12 with the lower wing sections so that both sides of the wings are identical.

23 Make 62 small rolls using one ⅛ x 2¼ in. (3 x 56mm) white strip joined with one ⅛ x 2¼ in. (3 x 56mm) black strip for each one.

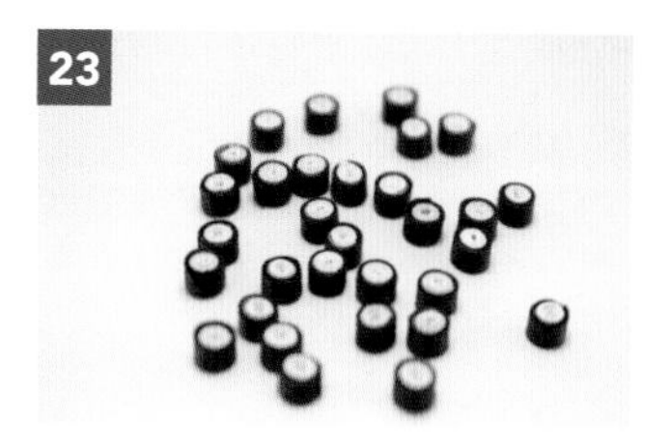

24 Glue these rolls along the side edges of all the wing sections.

25 Apply glue to one side of one ⅛ x 17¾ in. (3 x 450mm) black strip and attach it around the outline of one wing section. Cut off the excess strip and use it for another wing section. Use a second strip to outline the remaining two wing sections.

Making the body

26 Place the sheet of black A4 paper on the work surface so it is horizontal. Cut a triangular strip with a 2 in. (50mm) base and the width of the sheet of paper.

27 Roll up the strip, starting at the base (wide end) to make a tapering body which is broadest in the center.

Making the antennae

28 Fold one $\frac{1}{32}$ x $1\frac{9}{16}$ in. (1 x 40mm) black strip in half. Quill both ends to make small rolls and glue them in place.

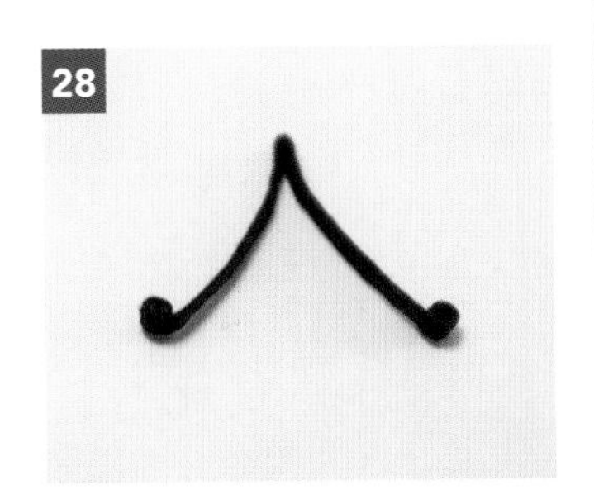

29 Glue the antennae to the top of the body.

Assembling all the sections

30 Glue the upper and lower wing sections together.

31 Glue the wings to the sides of the body.

Bumblebee

It's fascinating to watch a bumblebee fly from flower to flower to collect nectar and pollinate plants and listen to the buzz of its wings. These creatures are found all over the world and have come to represent hard work, family ties, and unity. Bees were sacred to the ancient Greek goddess Melissa, who was thought to have brought honey, rather than milk, to the god Zeus when he was a baby.

Getting started

First cut all your strips using a steel ruler and paper cutter on a cutting mat (see Techniques page 120). The Bumblebee has a thorax, abdomen, tail, and head; two antennae, six legs (two with pollen bags), two wings, and two eyes. The body is covered with fur.

- For the thorax you need two ⅛ x 11¾ in. (3 x 300mm) yellow strips and two ⅛ x 11¾ in. (3 x 300mm) black strips
- For the abdomen you need one 3⁄16 x 17¾ in. (5 x 450mm) black strip
- For the tail you need one ⅛ x 6 in. (3 x 150mm) black strip
- For the head and antennae you need one 1⁄32 x 9¾ in. (1 x 250mm) and one ⅛ x 9¾ in. (3 x 250mm) black strip, and one 1⁄32 x ¾ in. (1 x 20mm) hard black paper strip
- For the legs you need six 1⁄32 x 19⁄32 in. (1 x 15mm) hard black paper strips, six 1⁄32 x 11⁄16 in. (1 x 17mm) hard black paper strips, twelve 1⁄32 x 9⁄16 in. (1 x 40mm) black paper strips, and one ⅛ x 11¾ in. (3 x 300mm) yellow strip
- For the fur you need one ⅛ x 11¾ in. (3 x 300mm) yellow strip, one ⅛ x 11¾ in. (3 x 300mm) black strip, and one ⅛ x 6 in. (3 x 150mm) white strip
- For the wings you need two 1⁄32 x 11¾ in. (1 x 300mm) light brown strips
- For the eyes you need two 1⁄32 x 2 in. (1 x 50mm) black strips and two 1⁄32 x 7⁄16 in. (1 x 10mm) white strips
- For the pollen bags you need four 1⁄24 x 19⁄16 in. (1.5 x 40mm) yellow strips

You will need

Yellow paper strips:
3 strips ⅛ x 11¾ in. (3 x 300mm)
1 strip 1⁄32 x 2 in. (1 x 50mm)
4 strips 1⁄24 x 19⁄16 in. (1.5 x 40mm)

Black paper strips:
3 strips ⅛ x 11¾ in. (3 x 300mm)
1 strip 3⁄16 x 17¾ in. (5 x 450mm)
1 strip ⅛ x 6 in. (3 x 150mm)
1 strip 1⁄32 x 9¾ in. (1 x 250mm)
1 strip ⅛ x 9¾ in. (3 x 250mm)
12 strips 1⁄32 x 19⁄16 in. (1 x 40mm)
2 strips 1⁄32 x 2 in. (1 x 50mm)

Hard black paper strips:
1 strip 1⁄32 x ¾ in. (1 x 20mm)
6 strips 1⁄32 x 19⁄32 in. (1 x 15mm)
6 strips 1⁄32 x 11⁄16 in. (1 x 17mm)

White paper strips:
1 strip ⅛ x 6 in. (3 x 150mm)
2 strips 1⁄32 x 7⁄16 in. (1 x 10mm)

Light brown paper strips:
2 strips 1⁄32 x 11¾ in. (1 x 300mm)

Steel ruler
Paper cutter
Cutting mat
Paper clip
Sharp pair of scissors
Quilling tool
Mini Mold
Glue
Paintbrush
Needle tool

Finished size

Approximately 19⁄16 in. (40mm) long

Difficulty level

Advanced

Making the body

1 Take two ⅛ x 11¾ in. (3 x 300mm) yellow strips, and cut a fine fringe along one edge with sharp scissors (see Techniques page 123). Quill this strip into a tight roll.

2 Quill two ⅛ x 11¾ in. (3 x 300mm) black strips into a roll. Shape the roll into a dome using a Mini Mold (see Techniques page 125) as shown in the photograph. Glue from the inside and let dry.

3 Shape the fringed yellow roll into a dome and glue from the inside. Let dry. Glue the flat end of the yellow dome to the concave end of the black dome to make the thorax.

4 To make the abdomen, quill one 1¼ x 17¾ in. (5 x 450mm) black strip and make a roll. Use your finger to push the roll outward to make an elongated shape. Glue the inside and let dry.

1

2

3

4

5 Use glue to attach the abdomen to the back of the thorax.

6 Take one ⅛ x 11¾ in. (3 x 300mm) black strip, one ⅛ x 6 in. (3 x 150mm) white strip, and one ⅛ x 11¾ in. (3 x 300mm) yellow strip. Use a pair of scissors to cut a fringe along one long edge of each of them. Hold the other long edge of the strip in a clip to prevent you from cutting into it.

7 Glue the black fringed strip around the body starting at the point where the yellow fringed roll ends and so that the fringes overlap the previous fringes. Only fill one section of the body with the black fringed strip. Cut off the rest of the strip.

8 Repeat step 7 using the yellow fringed strip and starting at the point where the black fringed strip ended. Fill one section of the body with the yellow fringed strip. Cut off the rest of the strip.

5

6

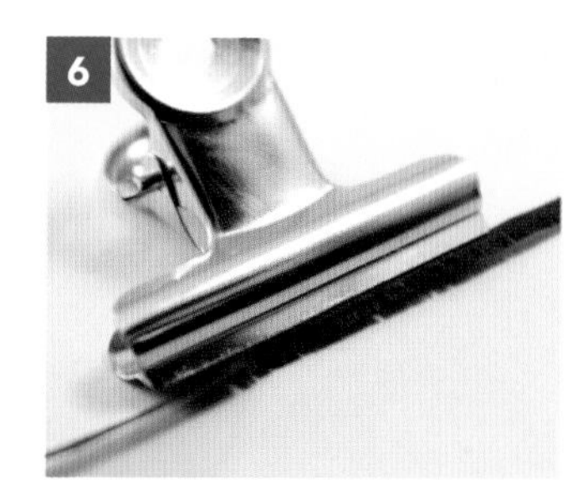

7

8

9 Repeat steps 7 and 8, filling one section of the body with the black strip and a second section with the yellow strip.

Making the tail

10 Make a roll using one ⅛ x 6 in. (3 x 150mm) black strip. Use your fingers to push the roll into a pointed dome. Glue it from the inside and let dry.

11 Glue the tail to the back of the abdomen. Cover the tail with the white fringed strip as shown in step 7, working to the tip.

Making the head

12 Quill one ⅛ x 9¾ in. (3 x 250mm) black paper strip into a roll. Push the roll outward using your fingers or any tool to create a cone shape as shown in the photograph. Quill one 1/32 x 9¾ in. (1 x 250mm) black paper strip into a roll.

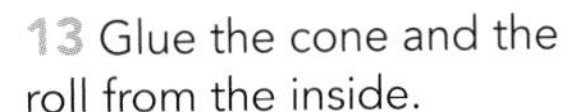

13 Glue the cone and the roll from the inside.

14 Glue the roll to the back of the cone so that the roll is at an angle to make the head.

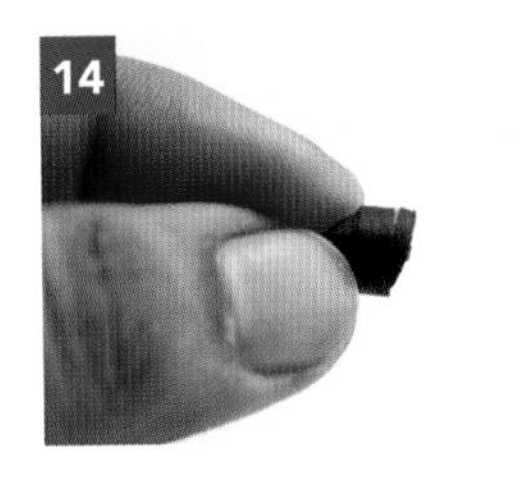

15 Glue the head to the front of the body.

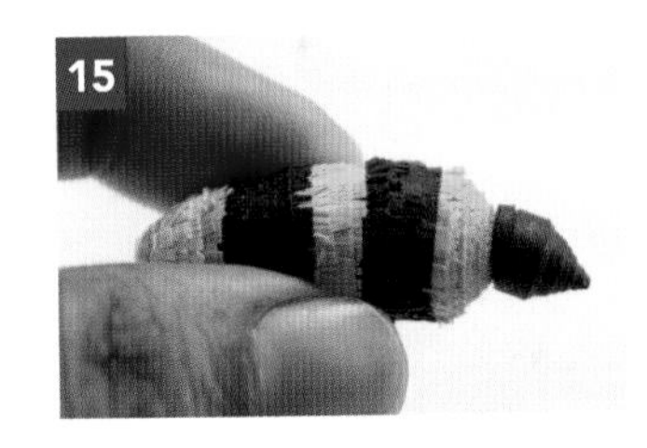

16 For each eye, quill one 1/32 x 1⅞ in. (1 x 50mm) black strip.

Making the wings

17 Quill one 1/32 x 11¾ in. (1 x 300mm) light brown paper strip.

18 Loosen the roll and press it into a leaf shape.

19 Press the leaf shape from two points to make a wing, as shown in the photograph (see Techniques page 122). Glue the back of the wing and let dry. Repeat steps 17 to 19 to make a second wing that is a mirror image of the first.

20 Apply glue to the pointed ends of the wings and attach them onto the body, fanning the wings upward. Glue the eyes to the head.

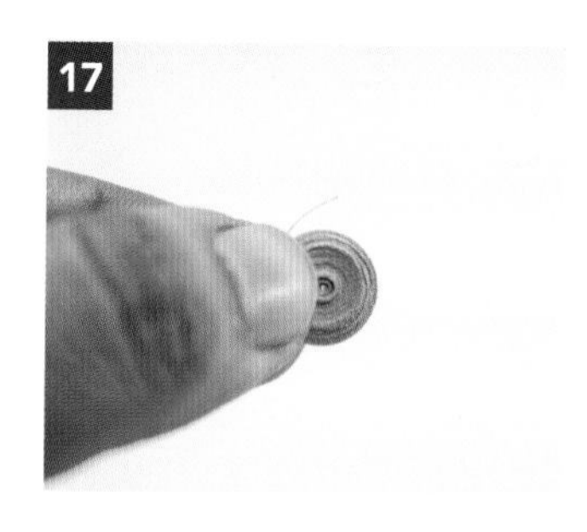
17

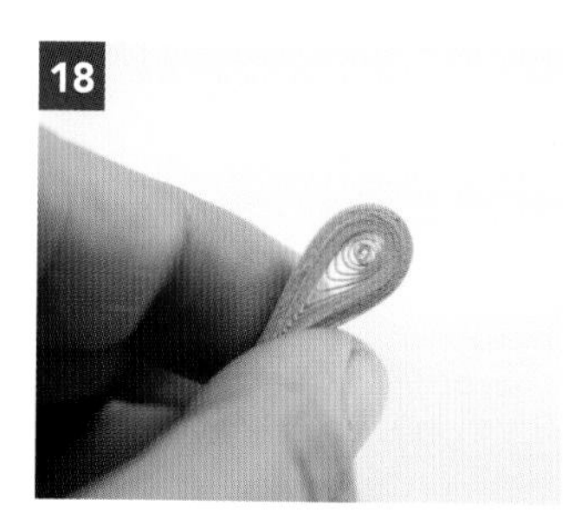
18

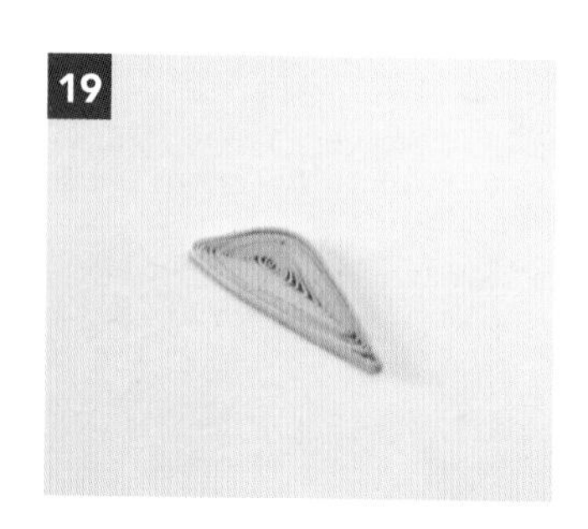
19

20

Making the legs

21 Quill one 1/32 x 9/16 in. (1 x 40mm) black paper strip into a roll and loosen it.

22 Now press the loosened roll from both ends and glue at the back. Repeat steps 21 and 22 to make a second roll.

23 Glue the two rolls to one 1/32 x 19/32 in. (1 x 15mm) hard black paper strip, leaving a 1/32 in. (1mm) gap between them and at least a ⅛ in. (3mm) strip at the end.

24 Cover the two rolls with a 1/32 x 11/16 in. (1 x 17mm) hard black paper strip so that the end of the hard strip is aligned with the base. Repeat steps 21 to 24 to make six legs.

25 Glue one end of the 1/32 x 2 in. (1 x 50mm) yellow strip around the 1/32 in. (1mm) gap between the two rolls. Cut off the excess and use it for the other legs.

26 Glue the legs to the body as shown in the photograph.

21

22

23

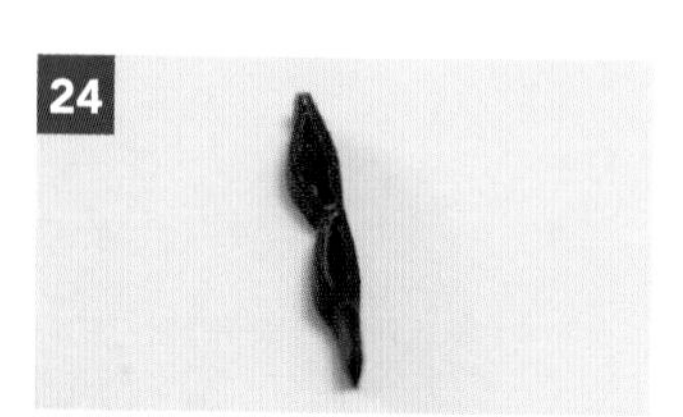
24

25

26

Making the antennae

27 Fold one 1/32 x 3/4 in. (1 x 20mm) hard black paper strip in half.

28 Glue it to the head as shown in the photograph.

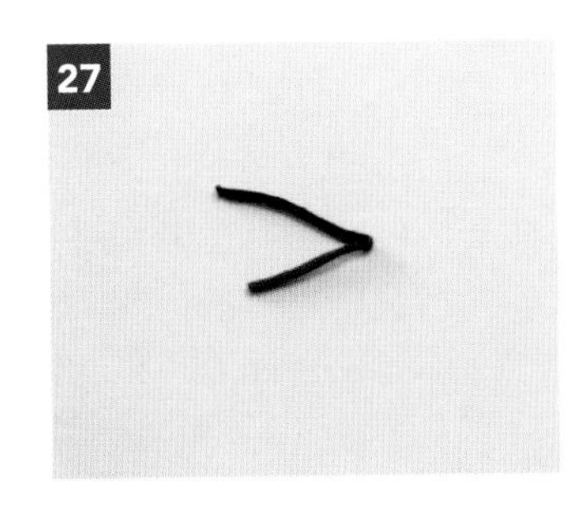

Making the pollen bags

29 Quill one 1/24 x 1 9/16 in. (1.5 x 40mm) yellow strip into a dome either on the quilling tool itself (by tilting the strip a little) or by first quilling it into a roll and then pressing it into a dome using any thin tool. Repeat to make four domes. Glue them from the inside and let dry.

30 Glue the rim of one dome to the rim of another to make one pollen bag. Repeat to make a second bag.

31 Glue the pollen bags on the hind legs.

32 Glue one 1/32 x 7/16 in. (1 x 10mm) white strip around the edge of each eye.

Dragonfly

In China, the dragonfly's darting flight is said to represent unpredictability. The Norse believed that the goddess Freya had dragonflies as her spirit guides. In other cultures, they symbolize peace, harmony, and purity. Dragonflies come in a variety of colors including blue, green, yellow, and red. They live in most parts of the world, but they prefer to live near ponds or streams.

Getting started

First cut all your strips using a steel ruler and paper cutter on a cutting mat (see Techniques page 120). The dragonfly has four wings, a body and head, six legs, two antennae, and two eyes.

- For the wings you need four ⅛ x 11¾ in. (3 x 300mm) graduated (shaded) strips
- For the body you need one A4 sheet and one 1/32 x 1⅞ x 11¾ in. (1 x 50 x 300mm) strip of brown paper
- For the head you need two 1/32 x 9¾ in. (1 x 250mm) brown strips
- For the legs you need six 1/32 x 19/32 in. (1 x 15mm) hard black paper strips
- For the antennae you need one 1/32 x ¾ in. (1 x 18mm) hard black paper strip
- For the eyes you need one 1-in. (25mm) square white paper

You will need

Graduated (shaded) paper strips:
4 strips ⅛ x 11¾ in. (3 x 300mm)

Brown paper strips:
2 strips 1/32 x 9¾ in. (1 x 250mm)

Hard black paper strips:
6 strips 1/32 x 19/32 in. (1 x 15mm)
1 strip 1/32 x ¾ in. (1 x 18mm)

Brown paper:
1 A4 size sheet

White paper:
1 1-in. (25mm) square

Steel ruler
Paper cutter
Cutting mat
Quilling comb
Crimping tool
Mini Mold
Glue
Paintbrush
Needle tool
Sharp pair of scissors

Finished size

Approximately 2¼ in. (55mm) long

Difficulty level

Easy

Making the wings

1 Crimp one ⅛ x 11¾ in. (3 x 300mm) graduated (shaded) paper strip using a paper crimper. Fold over 3/16 in. (5mm) of the dark shaded end of the strip and place it behind the prongs of the quilling comb (see Techniques page 124). Loop the 3/16 in. (5mm) fold onto the first prong of the comb, then bring the strip in front from the third prong.

2 Loop the strip onto the first prong again and then, from the back of the comb, bring the strip to the front from the fourth prong.

3 Repeat steps 1 and 2 until you reach the ninth prong. Glue the end of the strip in place.

4 Carefully slide the coils from the comb and press them together at the base. Apply glue on the back of the coils to keep them in place.

5 Repeat steps 1 to 4 to make four wing sections. Glue two sections together to make a pair of wings.

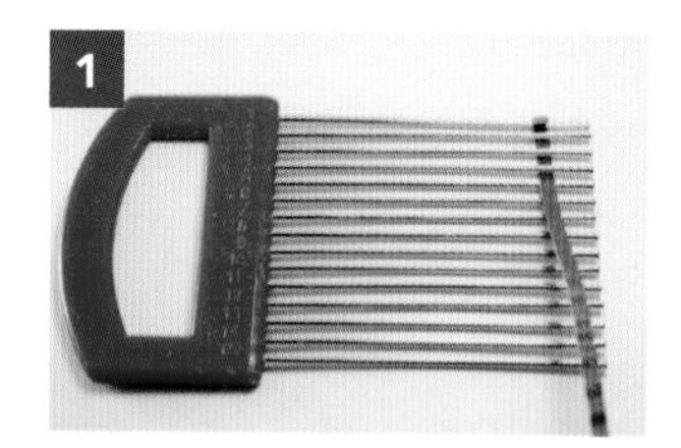

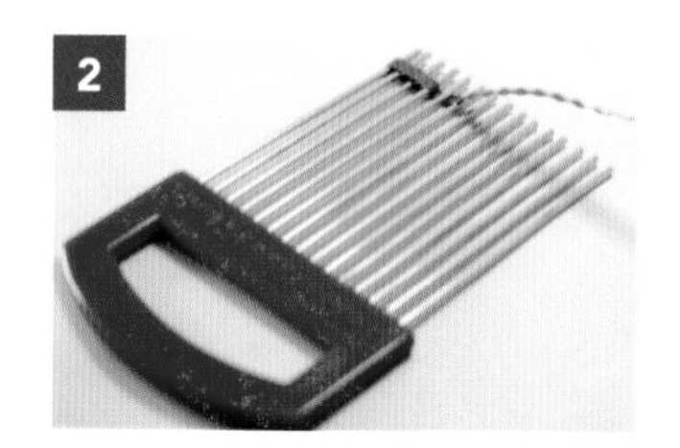

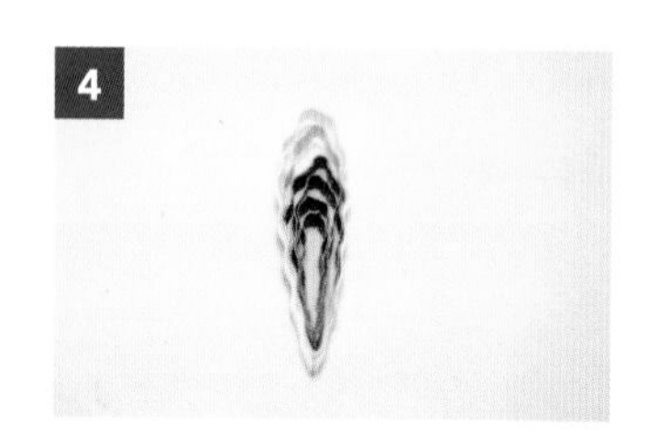

Making the body

6 Place the sheet of brown paper on a cutting mat so that it is horizontal. At the top of the piece of paper, mark a point 1 9/16 in. (40mm) from the right-hand edge. Position the ruler at an angle so that it is 1/32 in. (1mm) from the right-hand edge at the bottom of the sheet.

7 Use a paper cutter to cut along the ruler to cut out a triangle.

8 Starting at the wide end, roll the strip so that it is even at the top and tapered at the base. Roll until about 5½ in. (140mm) of the paper has been rolled.

9 Continue to roll up the paper, tapering a little at the top, until all of the paper triangle has been used.

10 The finished body will be broader at the top and narrower at the bottom.

Making the head

11 Quill two 1/32 x 9¾ in. (1 x 250mm) brown paper strips to make two identical rolls (see Techniques page 121). Shape them into a dome. Glue from the inside and let dry. Glue the domes together to make the head.

12 Glue the head to the top of the body.

Making the legs

13 Fold one 1/32 x 19/32 in. (1 x 15mm) strip of hard black paper at points ⅛ in. (3mm), ¼ in. (6mm), and ¼ in. (6mm) from one end. Repeat with five more strips of 1/32 x 19/32 in. (1 x 15mm) hard black paper.

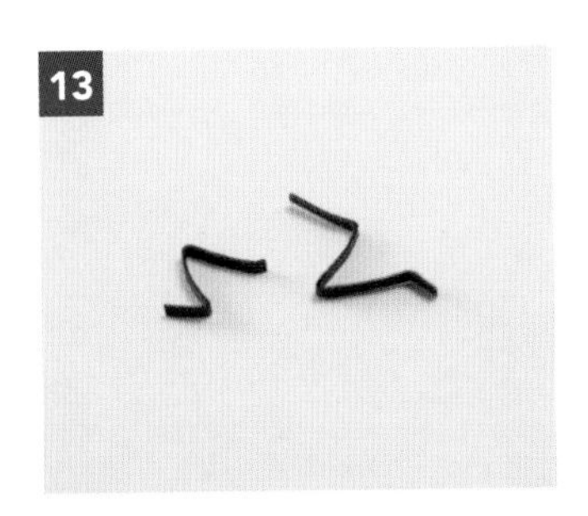

14 Glue three strips to each side of the body as shown in the photograph.

Making the antennae

15 Fold one 1/32 x ¾ in. (1 x 18mm) strip of black hard paper in half.

Assembling the dragonfly

16 Glue the antennae to the front of the head. Glue the wings to the sides of the body. Cut out two dots from white paper and glue to the head to make the eyes.

Birds

Intricately cut paper feathers help give a naturalistic finish to this flock of birds. The quilled paper bodies are covered with layers of colorful plumage. Finishing touches for the owl, peacock, parrot, and kingfisher include extravagant wings.

Kingfisher

The kingfisher has been a symbol of peace and prosperity in China for centuries. In America, the native tribes on the northwest coast viewed this bird as a messenger and a sign of good luck to come, while for the Siouan tribes it was associated with fertility. In traditional Native American stories, it frequently appears as a proficient hunter, whose success cannot be copied by careless imitators.

Getting started

First cut all your strips using a steel ruler and paper cutter on a cutting mat (see Techniques page 120). The kingfisher has one body, one head, two legs, one beak, two eyes, and multiple feathers.

- For the body you need fifty-one 3⁄16 x 11¾ in. (5 x 300mm) orange strips
- For the face you need nineteen 3⁄16 x 11¾ in. (5 x 300mm) orange strips
- For the legs and feet you need two ⅛ x 4 in. (3 x 100mm) and eight ⅛ x 1 9⁄16 in. (3 x 40 mm) reddish orange strips
- For the beak you need one ¼ x 13 in. (7 x 330mm) dark gray strip
- For the feathers you need A4 sheets of light blue, cobalt blue, dark blue, and yellow paper
- For the eyes you need A4 sheets of black, dark brown, and white paper

You will need

Orange paper strips:
70 strips 3⁄16 x 11¾ in. (5 x 300mm)

Reddish orange paper strips:
2 strips ⅛ x 4 in. (3 x 100mm)
8 strips ⅛ x 1 9⁄16 in. (3 x 40 mm)

Dark gray paper strips:
1 strip ¼ x 13 in. (7 x 330mm)

Light blue, cobalt blue, dark blue, yellow, black, dark brown, and white paper:
1 A4-size sheet of each color

Flexible metal wire (see page 119):
8 pieces

Steel ruler
Paper cutter
Cutting mat
Quilling tool
Glue
Paintbrush
Mini Mold
Sharp pair of scissors
Paper knife
Wire cutting tool
Needle tool

Finished size

Approximately 6¼ in. (16cm) long

Difficulty level

Moderate

Making the body

1 Make a roll using twenty-five orange 3/16 x 11¾ in. (5 x 300mm) strips (see Techniques page 121). Use your fingers to shape it into a cone 2 19/32 in. (60mm) high. Glue from the inside and let dry.

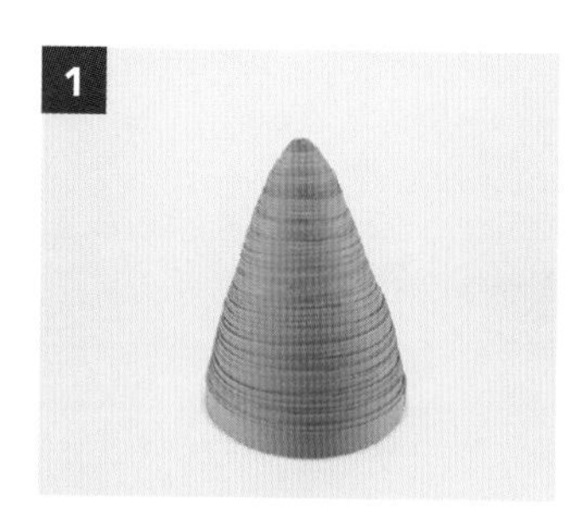

2 Make a second roll using twenty-six orange 3/16 x 11¾ in. (5 x 300mm) strips. Use your fingers to shape it into a cone 1 9/16 in. (40mm) high.

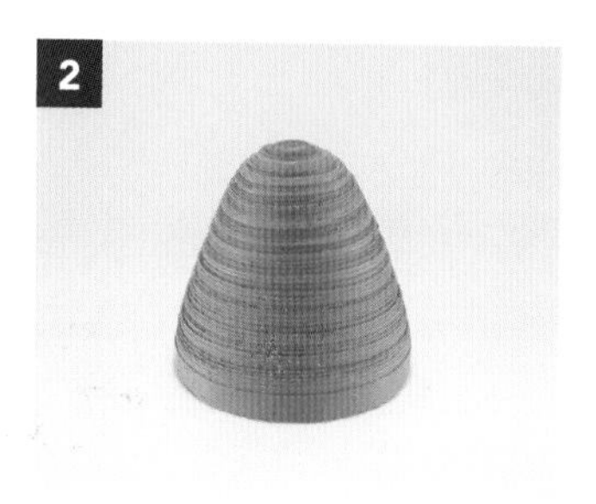

3 Press the tip of the cone on one side to create a tilted depression in the dome. Glue from the inside and let dry.

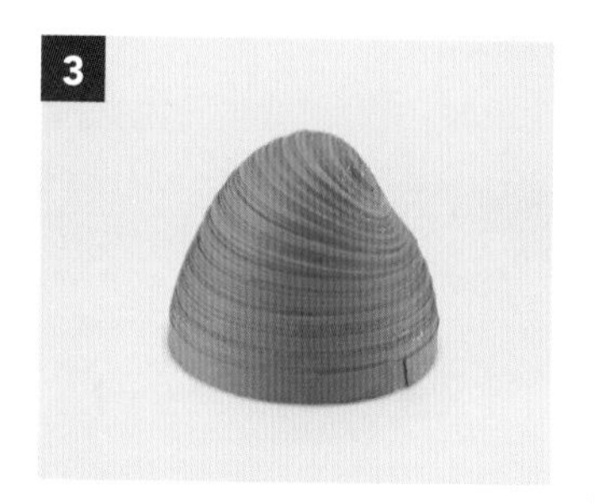

4 Glue the two cones together as shown in the photograph to make the body.

5 Make a roll using nine orange 3/16 x 11¾ in. (5 x 300mm) strips. Use your fingers to shape it into a cone 1 3/8 in. (30mm) high. Press the tip of the cone downward to create the shape shown in the photograph. Glue from the inside and let dry.

6 Make a roll using ten orange 3/16 x 11¾ in. (5 x 300mm) strips. Use your fingers to shape it into a cone ¾ in. (20mm) high. Glue from the inside and let dry.

7 Glue the shapes made in steps 5 and 6 together to make the head.

8 Glue the head to the depression in one end of the body.

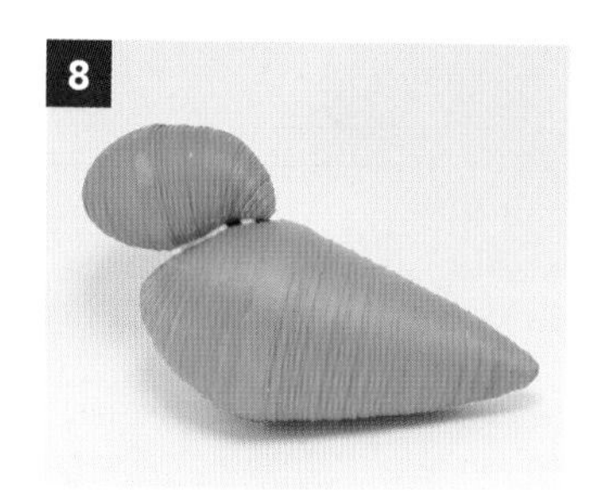

Making the wings

9 Using the wing template on page 127 as a guide, cut out two wings from yellow paper, making sure they are 2¹⁹⁄₃₂ in. (60mm) long (see Techniques page 123). Make five cuts evenly spaced along the length of the wings, extending upward from the narrow tip.

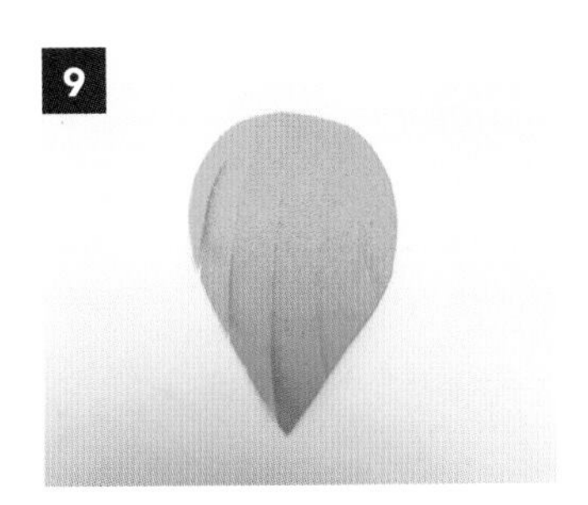

10 Using the wing feather template on page 127 as a guide, cut out fourteen shapes from the dark blue paper and sixty shapes from the cobalt blue paper. Use a sharp pair of scissors to cut a fringe in the tips of forty of the cobalt blue feathers. Set aside three fringed cobalt blue feathers for the tail.

11 Glue enough dark blue feathers to the tip of one of the wings to cover the yellow paper. Overlap the feathers and position them so they cover the tip of the wing.

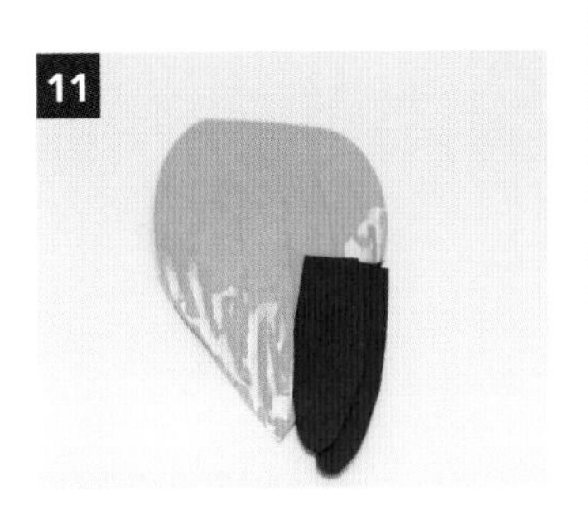

12 Continue to cover the wing with feathers, alternating cobalt and dark blue feathers and working up the wing as shown in the photograph. For the last three rows of feathers, glue on the fringed cobalt blue feathers.

13 Turn the wing over and trim the feathers that protrude below the yellow base so that they are rounded. Make four 7/16 in. (10mm) cuts in the rounded end of the wings.

14 Repeat steps 11 to 13 to make the second wing, ensuring it is a mirror image of the first wing. The completed wings should be about 3 in. (75mm) long.

Making the feathers

15 Using the long tail feathers template on page 127 as a guide, cut out six feather shapes from the light blue paper sheet. Use a sharp pair of scissors to cut a fringe along both long sides of the feathers, making sure you do not cut too close to the center (see Techniques page 123).

16 Glue three of the cobalt blue feathers made in step 10 to the tip of the body to start to make the tail. They should overlap and extend $\frac{13}{32}$–$\frac{3}{4}$ in. (10–20mm) from the tip of the body.

17 Glue on the light blue fringed feathers so that they overlap the cobalt blue feathers and the covering of feathers starts to extend up the body. Continue to glue overlapping light blue feathers along the center of the body until you reach the head.

18 Glue one wing to each side of the body, positioning them so that the tips touch the tail feathers.

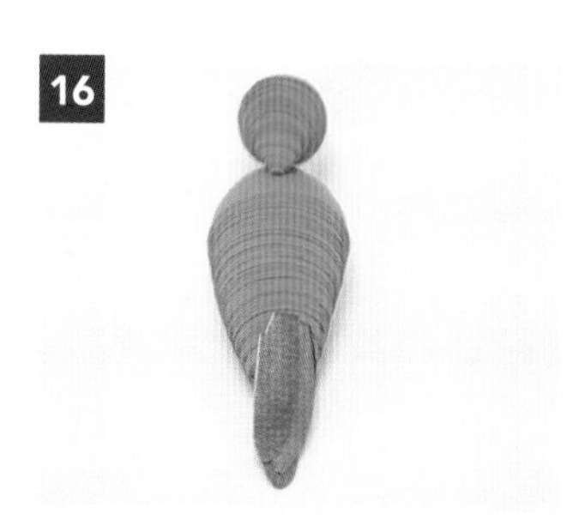

Decorating the head

19 Using the small and very small blue feathers template on page 127 as a guide, cut out forty small and eighty-five very small feather shapes from the cobalt blue paper (see Techniques page 123).

20 Using the rectangles template on page 127 as a guide, cut out two rectangles from the white paper. Starting at one end of the rectangles, glue the very small cobalt blue feathers to them. Continue until the rectangles are covered with feathers.

21 Glue the rectangles to the sides of the head, so that one end touches the wings

22 Using the small, medium, and large white feathers templates on page 127 as a guide, cut out sixty small, twenty medium, and ten large feathers from the white paper.

23 Glue the largest white feathers to the neck so that they overlap, followed by the medium-sized white feathers.

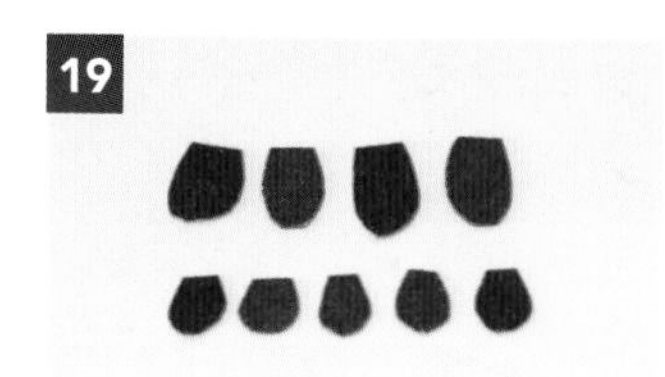

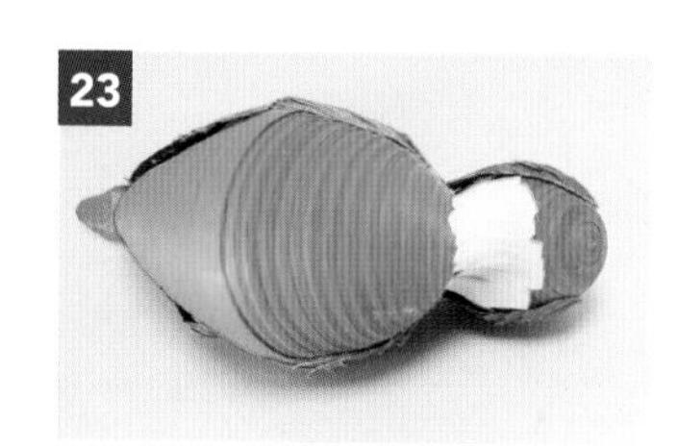

24 Make a roll using 1 dark gray ¼ x 13 in. (7 x 330mm) strip. Use your fingers to stretch it into a cone 1¾ in. (45mm) long. Glue it from the inside and let dry. Use a sharp pair of scissors to cut two short V-shapes into opposite sides of the wide end of the beak.

25 Glue the beak to the center-front of the head so that the uncut sides overlap the blue feathers attached in step 21.

26 Cover the rest of the neck with overlapping small white feathers. The feathers should extend to the beak.

27 Glue a patch of overlapping small white feathers to the back of the head, leaving a V-shaped gap between them. Glue some of the small cobalt blue feathers cut in step 19 in the space between the white feathers on the back of the head.

28 Cover the head with cobalt blue feathers, taking care not to cover all of the white feathers on the sides of the head.

29 Glue some more light blue feathers between the wings.

Making the feet and eyes

30 Make a roll from one reddish orange ⅛ x 4 in. (3 x 100mm) strip. Use your fingers to shape it into a cone $\frac{5}{16}$ in. (8mm) long. Repeat to make a second cone. Glue the cones from the inside and let dry.

31 On a quilling tool, quill one reddish orange ⅛ x 1$\frac{9}{16}$ in. (3 x 40 mm) strip into a cone. Repeat to make eight cones. Apply glue to the inside of each cone and insert a length of wire. Cut off the excess wire. Let dry. Glue three of these cones to the tip of the cone made in step 30 to make one leg and foot. Glue the fourth cone to the back of the leg (the cone made in step 30). Repeat to make the second foot.

32 Cut two tapered ovals from the sheet of black paper. Cut two smaller tapered ovals from the sheet of brown paper and glue to the black shapes. Cut two small disks from the sheet of white paper and glue in place to complete the eyes. Glue one eye to each side of the head.

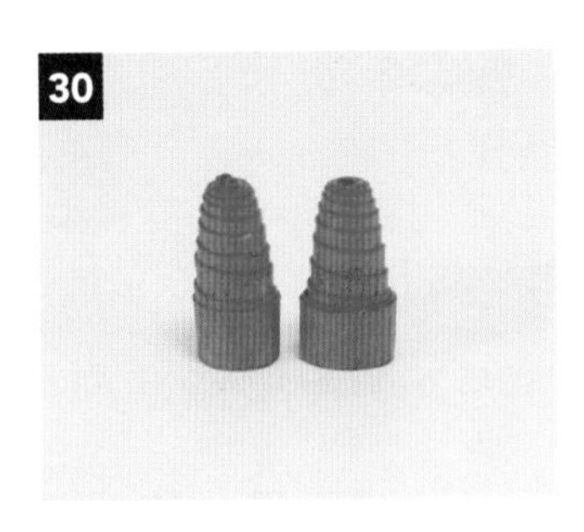

Tawny Owl

Owls have fascinated people for centuries. In ancient Greece and India, they represented wisdom and helpfulness. But in Europe during the Middle Ages, owls were associated with witches and the unknown, thanks to their eerie call, lonely appearance, and nocturnal habits. All this changed again during the eighteenth century, when scientific study encouraged people to overcome many superstitions.

Getting started

First cut all your strips using a steel ruler and paper cutter on a cutting mat (see Techniques page 120). The owl has one body, one head, two feet, and two wings.

- For the body you need thirty-five 3/16 x 11¾ in. (5 x 300mm) cream strips
- For the face you need twenty-three cream strips 3/16 x 11¾ in. (5 x 300mm) and one 3/16 x 1/32 x 11¾ in. (5 x 1 x 300mm) cream strip
- For the legs you need two 3/16 x 7 in. (5 x 180mm) and six ⅛ x 1 9/16 in. (3 x 40 mm) cream strips
- For the beak you need one ⅛ x 1 3/16 in. (3 x 30 mm) cream strip
- For the feathers you need ten 1/24 x 11¾ in. (1.5 x 300mm) and eighty 1/32 x 6 in. (1 x 150mm) dark brown paper strips and one hundred 1/32 x 6 in. (1 x 150mm) light brown paper strips
- For the eyes you need six 1/32 x 11¾ in. (1 x 300mm) and six 1/32 x 3 in. (1 x 75mm) white strips

You will need

Cream paper strips:
58 strips (3/16 x 11¾ in. (5 x 300mm)
1 strip 3/16 x 1/32 x 11¾ in. (5 x 1 x 300mm)
2 strips 3/16 x 7 in. (5 x 180mm)
6 strips ⅛ x 1 9/16 in. (3 x 40 mm)
1 strip ⅛ x 1 3/16 in. (3 x 30 mm)

Dark brown paper strips:
10 strips 1/24 x 11¾ in. (1.5 x 300mm)
80 strips 1/32 x 6 in. (1 x 150mm)

Light brown paper strips:
100 strips 1/32 x 6 in. (1 x 150mm)

White paper strips:
6 strips 1/32 x 11¾ in. (1 x 300mm)
6 strips 1/32 x 3 in. (1 x 75mm)

Dark brown, yellow, and black paper:
1 A4-size sheet of each color

Flexible metal wire (see page 119):
6 pieces

Steel ruler
Paper cutter
Cutting mat
Quilling tool
Mini Mold
Glue
Paintbrush
Needle tool
Sharp pair of scissors
Paper knife
Wire cutting tool

Finished size

Approximately 3¼ in. (85mm) high

Difficulty level

Moderate

Making the body and head

1 Make a roll using seventeen 3⁄16 x 11¾ in. (5 x 300mm) cream strips (see Techniques page 121). Use your fingers to extend it into a dome 1 7⁄16 in. (35mm) high (see Techniques page 125). Press the tip to flatten it. Make a second roll using eighteen 3⁄16 x 11¾ in. (5 x 300mm) cream strips. Use your fingers to extend it into a dome 1 in. (25mm) high. Glue the insides and let dry.

2 Glue the open ends of the domes together with the shorter one as the base. This will be the body.

3 Make a roll using eleven 3⁄16 x 11¾ in. (5 x 300mm) cream strips. Use your fingers to extend it into a dome 19⁄32 in. (15mm) high. Flatten the tip of the dome. Make a second dome using twelve 3⁄16 x 11¾ in. (5 x 300mm) cream strips but do not flatten it. Glue the insides of both domes and let dry. Glue the open ends of the domes together, with the flattened dome as the base. Glue to the body to make the head.

4 Glue one 3⁄16 x 1⁄32 x 11¾ in. (5 x 1 x 300mm) cream strip around the neck to cover the join.

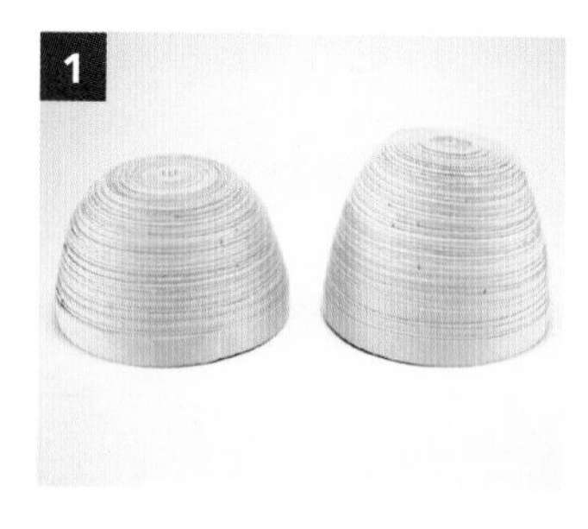

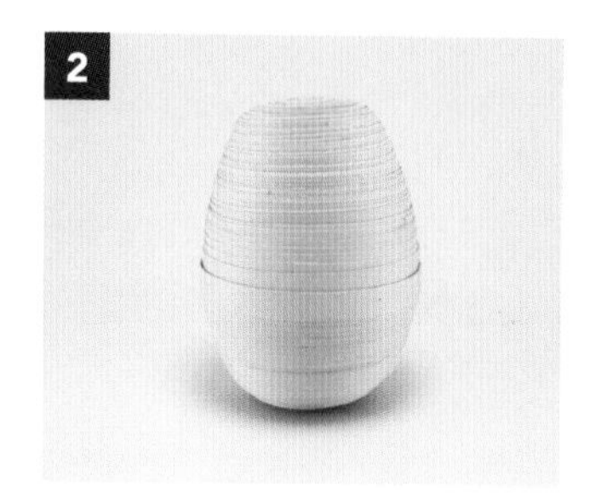

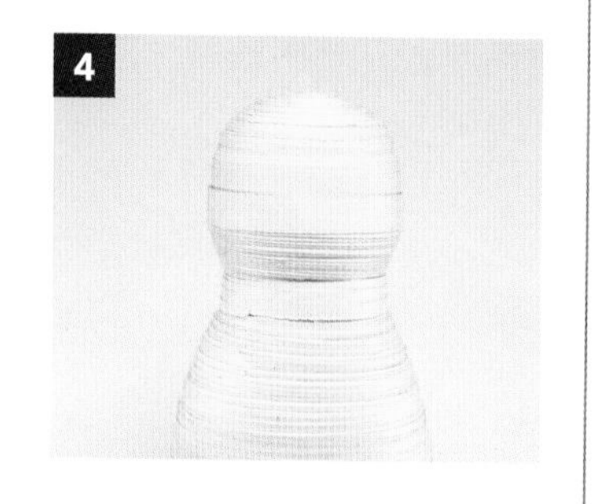

Making the feathers

5 Quill a 1⁄24 x 11¾ in. (1.5 x 300mm) dark brown strip into a roll and loosen it. Press it from one side to make a teardrop shape (see Techniques page 122). Repeat to make ten teardrop shapes.

6 Glue one side of the teardrop shapes made in step 5 at the bottom of the back of the body, as shown in the photograph, to make the tail.

7 Using the feather template on page 126 as a guide, cut out 250–300 shapes from the dark brown paper.

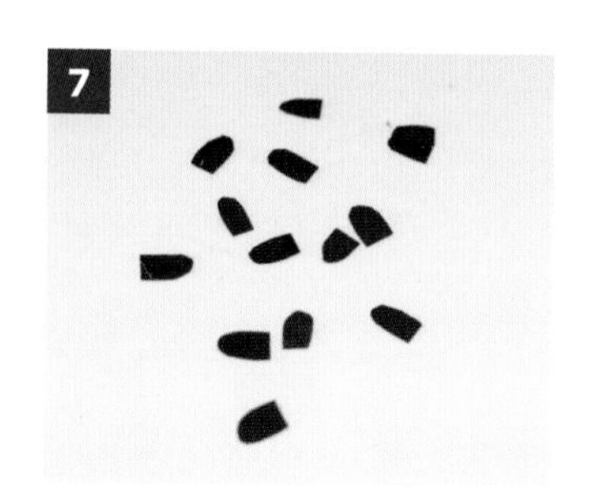

8 Glue the brown feathers to the body, starting $\frac{19}{32}$ in. (15mm) below the neck. Work upward toward the neck, positioning the feathers in a V-shape and so that they overlap.

9 Glue the feathers around the back of the neck as a continuation of the V-shape on the front of the body.

10 Continue to add feathers until the head is entirely covered.

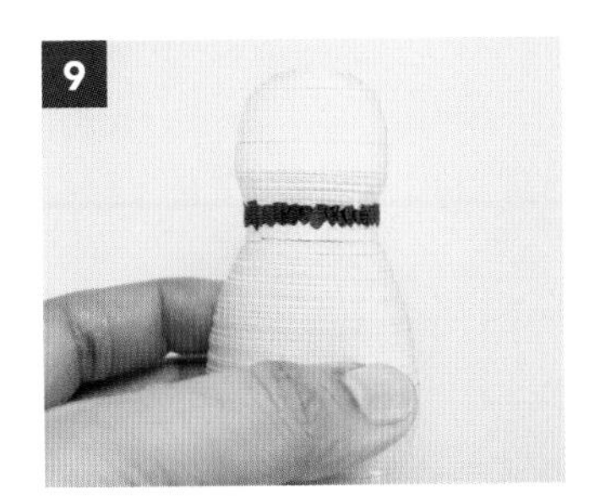

Making the eyes, beak, and eye feathers

11 Make a roll from three $\frac{1}{32}$ x $11\frac{3}{4}$ in. (1 x 300mm) white strips. Loosen the roll a little, press it from two sides and flatten it, as shown in the photograph. Make a second, similar shape. Glue the shapes from the back.

12 Cut two disks from the sheet of dark brown paper, two smaller disks from the sheet of yellow paper, and two tiny disks from the black paper. Glue the disks together to make the eyes.

13 Glue the eyes to the white rolls made in step 11 and as shown in the photograph.

14 Quill one $\frac{1}{8}$ x $1\frac{3}{16}$ in. (3 x 30 mm) cream strip on a quilling tool so that it is about $\frac{1}{4}$ in. (7mm) long.

15 Press the cone to make a curve. Glue from the inside.

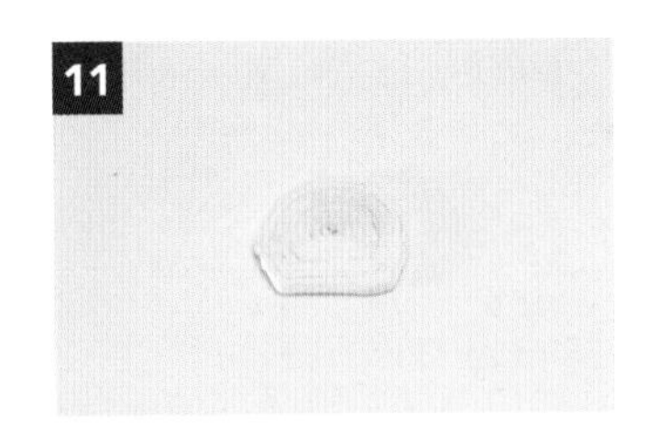

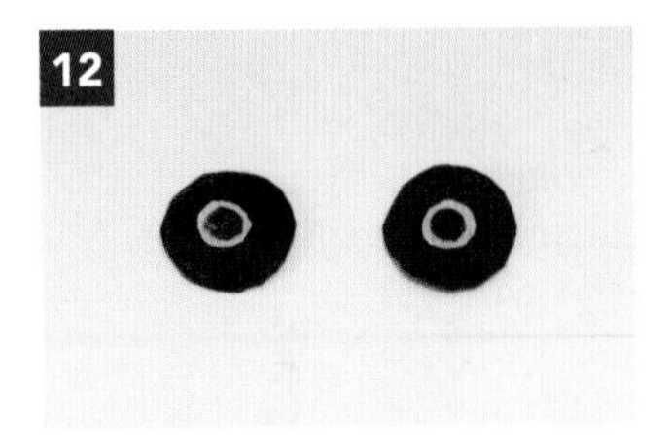

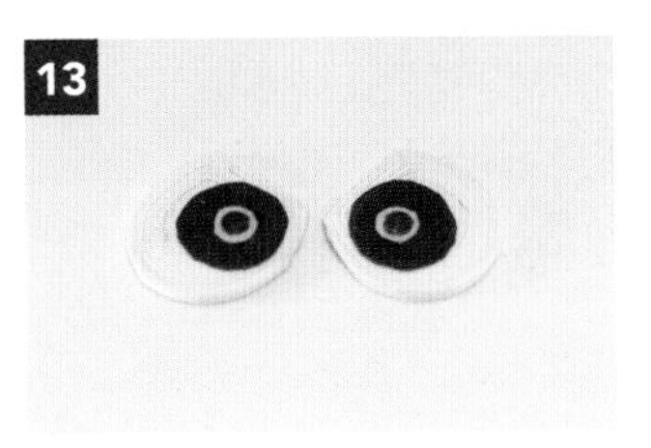

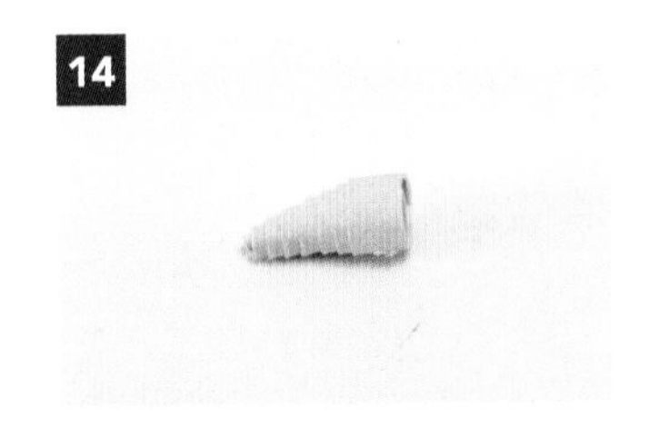

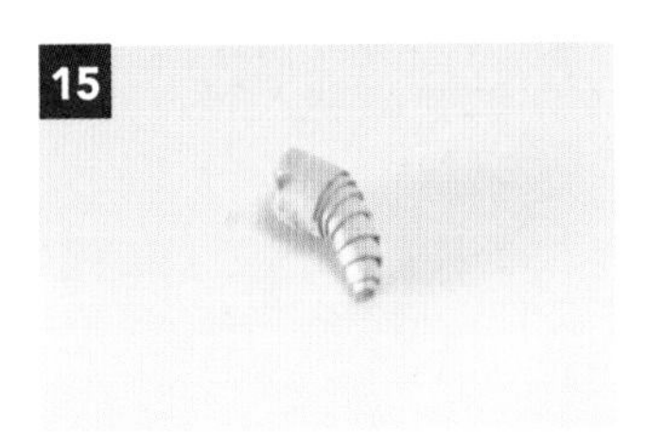

16 Glue the eyes to the head. Glue the cone between them to make the beak.

17 Quill one 1/32 x 3 in. (1 x 75mm) white strip and allow it to open as much as it can by itself.

18 Press the open coil into a teardrop shape (see Techniques page 122) and glue the end in place. Repeat steps 17 and 18 to make six teardrops.

19 Glue three teardrops together, one below the other, to make one eye feather. Repeat to make a second eye feather.

20 Glue a group of feathers above each eye.

Making the legs

21 Make two rolls, each one using one 3/16 x 7 in. (5 x 180mm) cream strip. Use your fingers to shape them into a cone 5/16 in. (8mm) high. Make six cones on the quilling tool, each one using one 1/8 x 1 9/16 in. (3 x 40 mm) cream strip.

22 Apply glue to the inside of the six smaller cones and insert a length of wire into each one. Cut off the excess wire. Let dry.

23 Curve the wired cones and glue three to the tip of each of the larger cones to make the legs. Shape the backs of the tops of the legs so that they fit against the body.

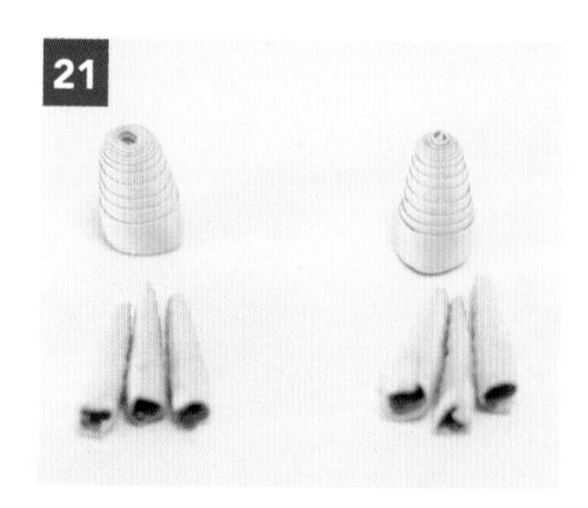

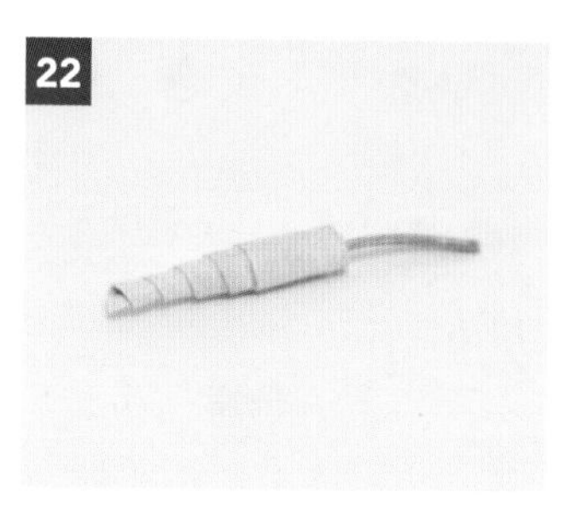

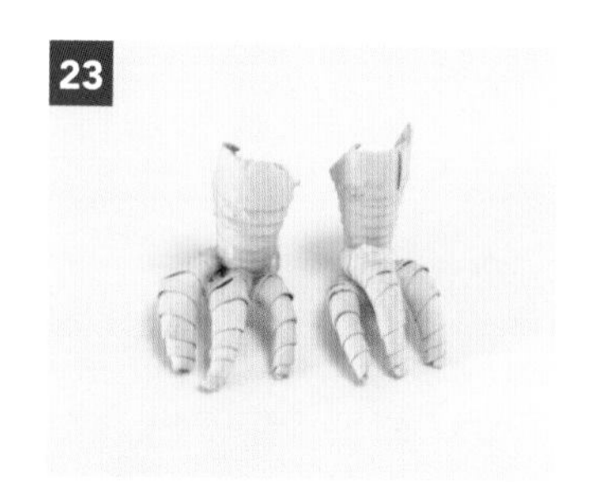

Making the wings

24 Using the template on page 127 as a guide, cut two wings from the brown paper (see Techniques page 123).

25 Use a pair of scissors to make seven evenly spaced cuts along the length of the wings, extending upward from the narrow tip.

26 Quill one 1/32 x 6 in. (1 x 150mm) dark brown strip. Open the roll and press it in a teardrop shape. Repeat to make eighty dark brown teardrops and one hundred light brown teardrops, using 1/32 x 6 in. (1 x 150mm) strips.

27 Glue a row of dark brown feathers along the lower edge of one of the wings.

28 Working upward and in rows, glue a mixture of dark and light brown feathers to the wing so that they overlap and fill the wing.

29 Repeat steps 27 and 28 to cover the second wing with feathers.

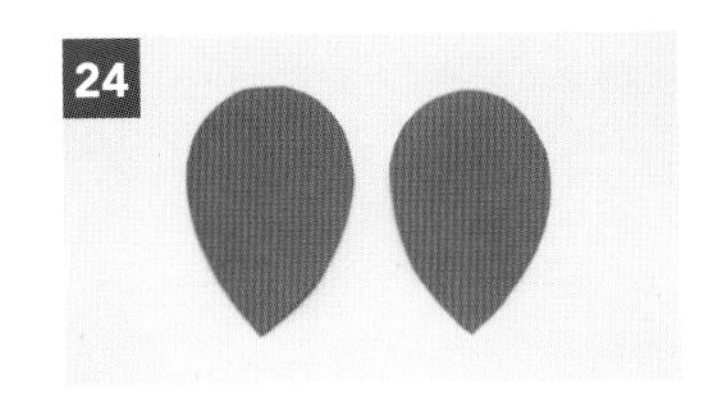

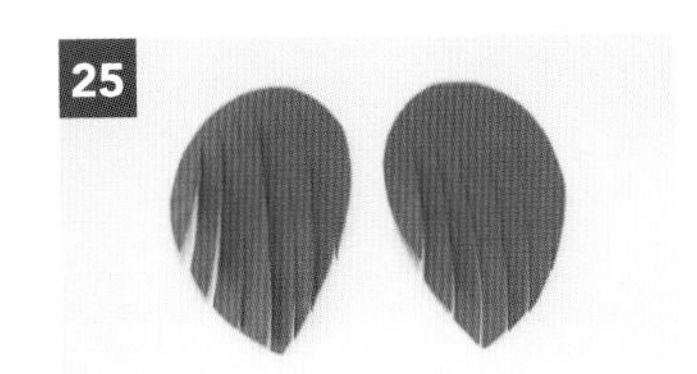

Assembling the wings and legs

30 Glue one wing to each side of the body. Glue the legs to the front of the body.

31 Check that the narrow ends of the wings touch the tail. Let dry.

Parrot

These colorful birds were traded by Native American tribes who imported them and their feathers from Mexico and other countries in the south of the continent. Parrot feathers have been found in the regalia of Plains Indian tribes, and wealthy people in the ancient Anasazi civilization kept them as pets. For some Pueblo tribes parrots are a fertility symbol.

Getting started

First cut all your strips using a steel ruler and paper cutter on a cutting mat (see Techniques page 120). The parrot has one body, one head, two legs, two wings, and multiple feathers.

- For the body you need thirty-one 3⁄16 x 11¾ in. (5 x 300mm) yellow strips
- For the face you need twelve 3⁄16 x 11¾ in. (5 x 300mm) yellow strips
- For the legs you need two 3⁄16 x 6 in. (5 x 150mm) yellow strips
- For the feet you need six 3⁄16 x ¾ in. (5 x 20mm) cream strips
- For the beak you need one 3⁄16 x 9¾ in. (5 x 250mm) dark brown strip
- For the feathers you need A4 sheets of green, navy blue, and yellow paper
- For the eyes and beak you need A4 sheets of black, white, and dark brown paper

You will need

Yellow paper strips:
43 strips 3⁄16 x 11¾ in. (5 x 300mm)
2 strips 3⁄16 x 6 in. (5 x 150mm)

Cream paper strips:
6 strips 3⁄16 x ¾ in. (5 x 20mm)

Dark brown paper strips:
1 strip 3⁄16 x 9¾ in. (5 x 250mm)

Green, navy blue, yellow, black, white, and dark brown paper:
1 A4-size sheet of each color

Flexible metal wire (see page 119):
6 pieces

Steel ruler
Paper cutter
Cutting mat
Quilling tool
Mini Mold
Glue
Paintbrush
Paper clip
Sharp pair of scissors
Paper knife
Wire cutting tool
Needle tool

Finished size

Approximately 6¼ in. (160mm) high

Difficulty level

Moderate

Making the body

1 Make a roll using fifteen 3/16 x 11¾ in. (5 x 300mm) yellow strips (see Techniques page 121). Shape it into a cone 2 in. (50mm) high (see Techniques page 125) and so that it has a slight curve. Glue the inside and let dry.

2 Make a second roll using sixteen 3/16 x 11¾ in. (5 x 300mm) yellow strips. Shape it into a dome 1 in. (25mm) high. Glue the inside and let dry.

3 Glue the open ends of the domes together to make the body.

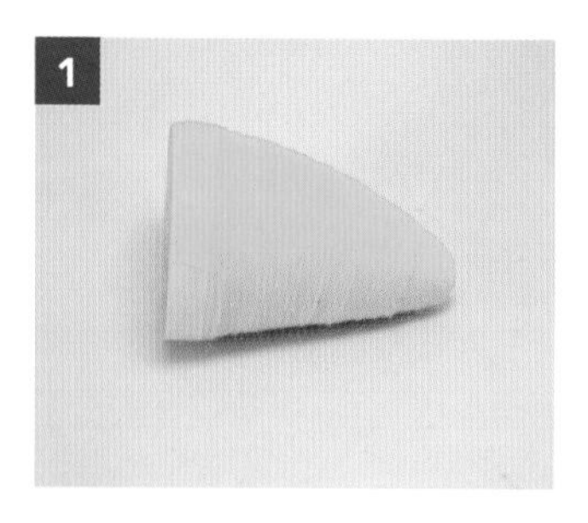

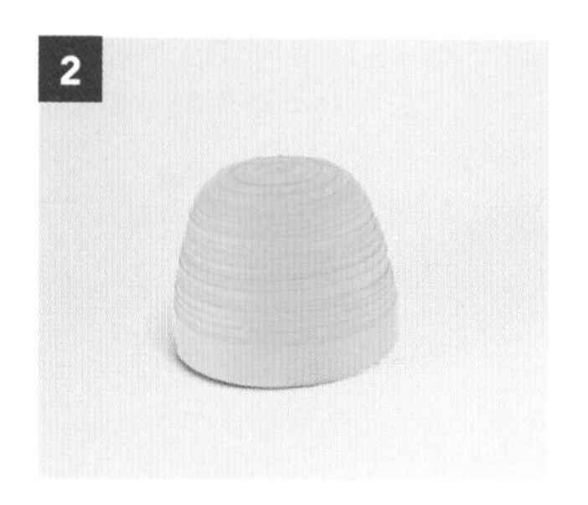

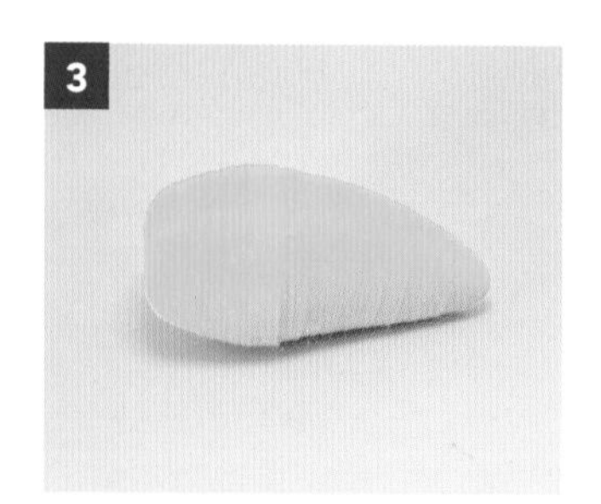

Making the face

4 Make a dome using twelve 3/16 x 11¾ in. (5 x 300mm) yellow strips. The dome should be about 1 3/16 in. (30mm) high.

5 Use your fingers to press one side of the top of the dome inward to create a depression as shown in the photograph. Glue from the inside and let dry.

6 Glue the dome to the top of the body as the head, keeping the curved part of the body facing downward.

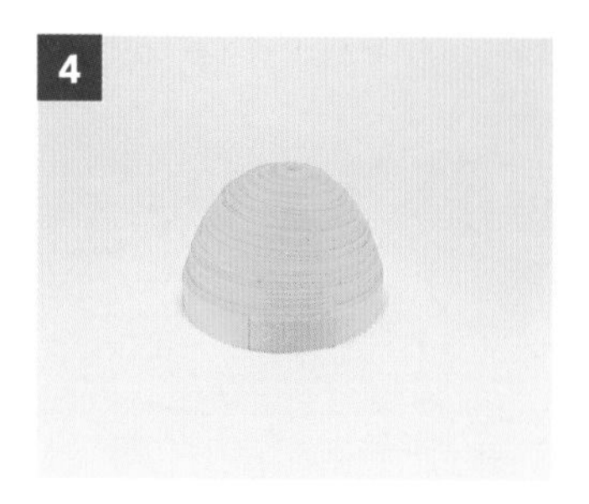

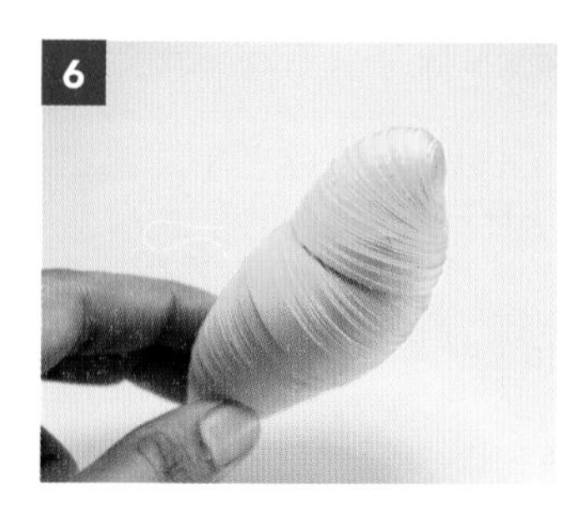

Making the tail

7 Using the tail feather template on page 126 as a guide, cut two green, two navy blue, and one yellow tail feather from the sheets of paper (see Techniques page 123).

8 Fold one of the feathers lengthwise and use a clip to hold the folded edge (see Techniques page 123).

9 Use a sharp pair of scissors to cut a fringe along the whole length of the feather. Remove the clip and open up the feather.

10 Repeat steps 8 and 9 for the remaining feathers.

11 Glue the two blue feathers on top of one another. Glue one green feather on top of them, followed by the yellow feather, and then the second green feather to make the tail.

12 Glue the tail to the bottom of the body, 19⁄32 in. (15mm) from the end.

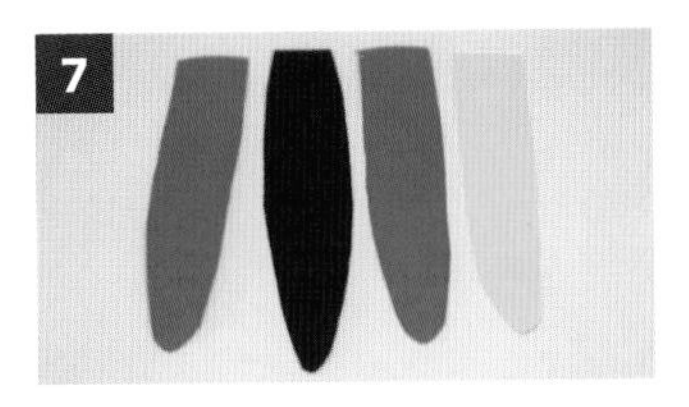

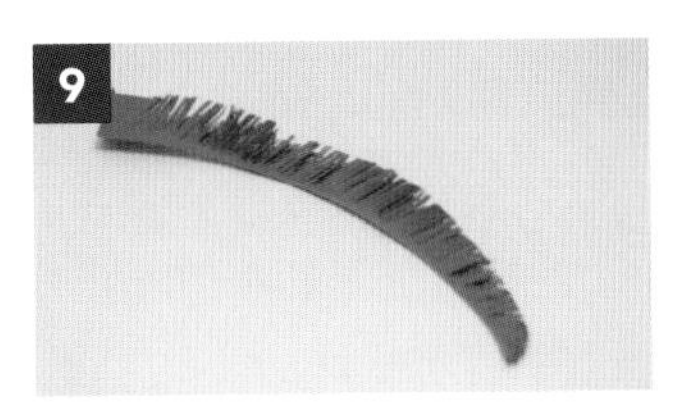

Making the feathers

13 Using the body feather templates on page 126 as a guide, cut out fifty-five green, eight navy blue, and eight yellow shapes of different sizes (see Techniques page 123).

14 Use a sharp pair of scissors to cut a deep fringe along the bottom of all the feathers.

15 Glue some green feathers in the middle part of the body so that they overlap the top of the tail. Make sure the feathers cover the point where the tail joins the body—only the fringes should be visible. Attach the bigger ones first, and then keep reducing the sizes of the feathers as you move upward to the point where the face starts.

16 Cover the middle part of the body, as far as the neck, with green feathers.

Making the wings

17 Using the template on page 126, cut out two wings from yellow paper. Using the template on page 126, cut out five navy blue wing feathers, five large yellow body feathers, six green medium-sized body feathers, and fifteen small green body feathers.

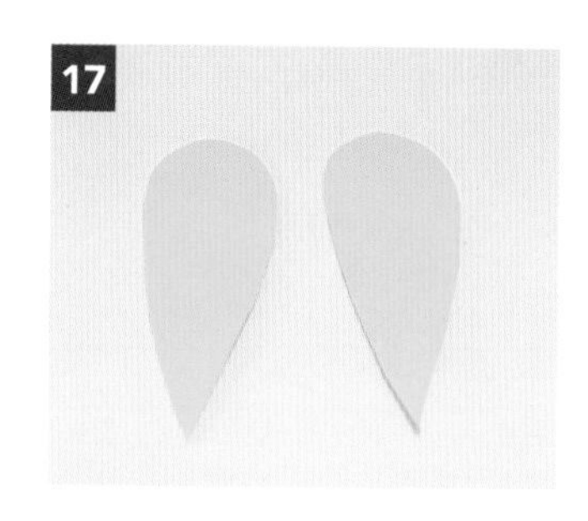

18 Start to cover the wings with feathers, beginning with the large navy blue feathers. Work on both the wings simultaneously to ensure they are a mirror image of each other.

19 Add three more rows of large navy blue feathers, working up the wings. Add green, yellow, and more navy blue feathers to the wings. Glue on smaller feathers as you work upward.

20 Cover the tops of the wings with small green feathers. The completed wings should be about 3⅛ in. (80mm) long.

21 Turn the wings over and fold under any green feathers that protrude from the edges of the wings so that the tops of the wings maintain their circular shape.

22 Glue one wing to each side of the body. The upper end should be aligned with the green body feathers and the tip should meet the top of the tail.

Making the eyes, beak, and feet

23 Cut two disks from the sheet of white paper and two tiny disks from the black paper. Glue the disks together to make the eyes. Glue one to each side of the head.

24 Make two rolls, each one using one 3⁄16 x 6 in. (5 x 150mm) yellow strip. Use the tip of a paintbrush handle to press them into a dome shape. Glue from the inside and let dry.

25 Quill one 3⁄16 x 9¾ in. (5 x 250mm) cream strip into a cone. Repeat to make six cones. Apply glue to the inside of the cones and insert a length of wire inside each of them. Cut off the excess wire and let dry.

26 Glue three cones to the base of each dome to make the legs and feet.

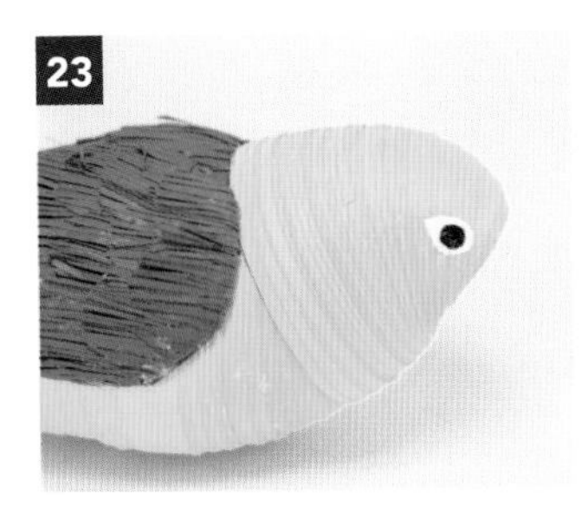
23

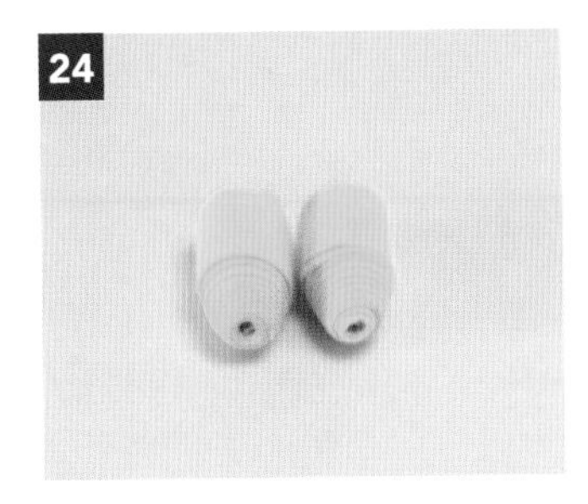
24

25

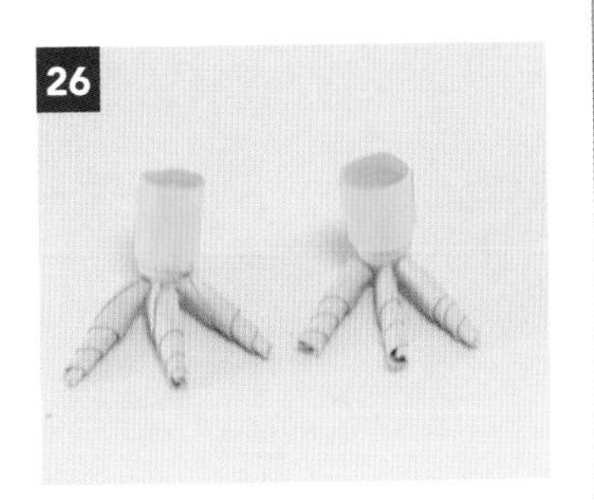
26

27 Glue the legs at the bottom of the body. Bend the feet into a curve.

28 Make a roll using one 3⁄16 x 9¾ in. (5 x 250mm) dark brown strip. Use a needle tool to elongate the roll and shape it in a narrow tapering cone about ½ in. (12mm) long. Glue from the inside.

29 Before the glue is completely dry, press the front part of the cone to make a deep curve.

30 Cut a half-moon shape, as shown in the photograph, from the dark brown paper. It should be wide enough to fit the sides of the cone made in steps 28 and 29.

31 Glue the curved cone in the depression created in the face. Glue the half-moon shape below the cone to complete the beak as shown in the photograph.

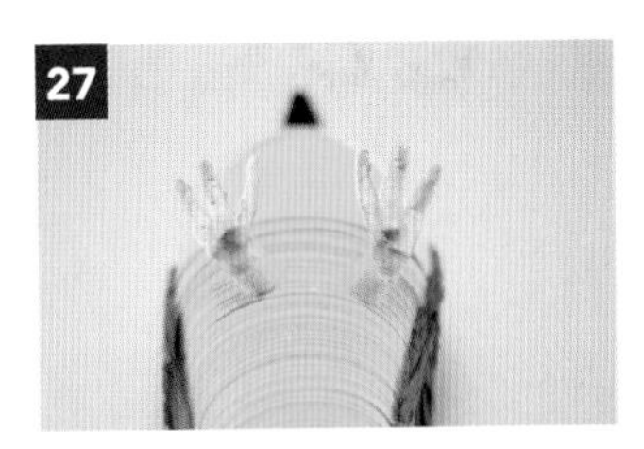
27

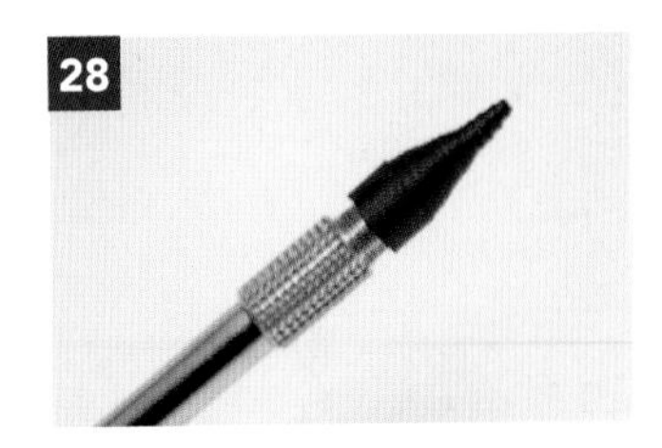
28

29

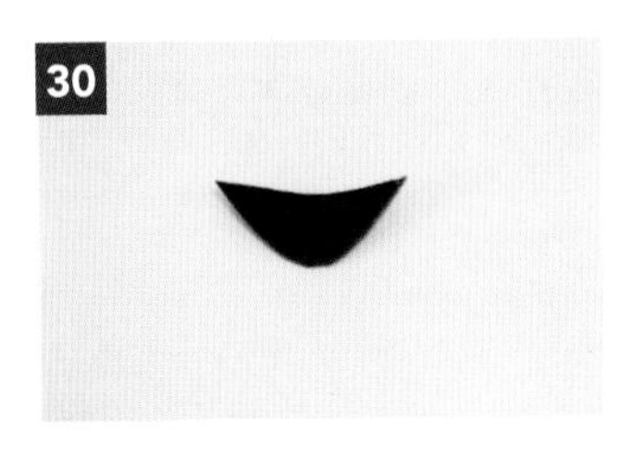
30

31

Peacock

The extravagant feathers of the male peacock have won it admirers around the world. It is the national bird of India, where keeping peacock feathers in the house is said to bring good luck, wealth, and prosperity. In Chinese mythology, its plumage is said to be a blend of five colors that create the harmony of sound. In ancient Egypt, peacocks were linked to the sun god, Amon-Ra, and the all-seeing eye of Horus.

Getting started

First cut all your strips using a steel ruler and paper cutter on a cutting mat (see Techniques page 120). The peacock has one head and body covered by multiple feathers, two legs, and a crown.

- For the body you need fifty-seven 3/16 x 11¾ in. (5 x 300mm) and two ⅛ x 11¾ in. (3 x 300mm) royal blue strips
- For feathers you need forty-one 1/32 x 3 in. (1 x 75mm) royal blue strips; forty-five 1/32 x 2¼ in. (1 x 55mm) light blue strips; thirty-six 1/32 x 3¾ in. (1 x 95mm) sea green strips; forty-nine 1/32 x 3¼ in. (1 x 85mm) green strips; thirty-six 1/32 x 2½ in. (1 x 65mm), thirty-one 1/32 x 1¾ in. (1 x 45mm), two hundred and forty-eight 1/32 x 7/16 in. (1 x 10mm), thirteen 1/32 x 1 9/16 in. (1 x 40mm), and fifty-two 1/32 x 11¾ in. (1 x 300mm) dark green strips; two 1/32 x 4 in. (1 x 100mm) turquoise strips; twenty-six 1/24 x 11¾ in. (1.5 x 300mm) hard white paper strips; and A4-size sheets of turquoise and green paper
- For the wings, eyes, and beak you need one A4 white and one A4 black sheet of paper
- For the crown you need seven 1/24 x ¾ in. (1.5 x 20mm) royal blue strips and seven 1/32 x 7/16 in. (1 x 10mm) hard white paper strips
- For the legs you need two 3/16 x 4 in. (5 x 100mm) and six 3/16 x 1 9/16 in. (5 x 40mm) cream strips

You will need

Royal blue paper strips:
57 strips 3/16 x 11¾ in. (5 x 300mm)
2 strips ⅛ x 11¾ in. (3 x 300mm)
41 strips 1/32 x 3 in. (1 x 75mm)
7 strips 1/24 x ¾ in. (1.5 x 20mm)

Light blue paper strips:
45 strips 1/32 x 2¼ in. (1 x 55mm)

Sea green paper strips:
36 strips 1/32 x 3¾ in. (1 x 95mm)

Green paper strips:
49 strips 1/32 x 3¼ in. (1 x 85mm)

Dark green paper strips:
36 strips 1/32 x 2½ in. (1 x 65mm)
31 strips 1/32 x 1¾ in. (1 x 45mm)
248 strips 1/32 x 7/16 in. (1 x 10mm)
13 strips 1/32 x 1 9/16 in. (1 x 40mm)
52 strips 1/32 x 11¾ in. (1 x 300mm)

Turquoise paper strips:
2 strips 1/32 x 4 in. (1 x 100mm)

Cream paper strips:
2 strips 3/16 x 4 in. (5 x 100mm)
6 strips 3/16 x 1 9/16 in. (5 x 40mm)

Hard white paper strips:
26 strips 1/24 x 11¾ in. (1.5 x 300mm)
7 strips 1/32 x 7/16 in. (1 x 10mm)

Turquoise, green, white, and black paper:
1 A4-size sheet of each color

Steel ruler
Paper cutter
Cutting mat
Quilling tool
Mini Mold
Glue
Paintbrush
Needle tool
Sharp pair of scissors
Paper knife
Circle punching machine

Finished size

Approximately 9½ in. (24cm) long

Difficulty level

Advanced

Making the body

1 Make a roll using twenty-five 3/16 x 11¾ in. (5 x 300mm) royal blue strips (see Techniques page 121). Use your fingers to shape the roll into a cone 2¼ in. (55mm) high (see Techniques page 125). Press the tip of the dome downward to make a curve and so that the cone is 2 in. (50mm) high. Glue the inside and let dry.

2 Make a roll using twenty-six 3/16 x 11¾ in. (5 x 300mm) royal blue strips. Use your fingers to shape the roll into a cone 2¼ in. (55mm) high. Press the tip of the dome upward to make a deep curve and so that the cone is 1¾ in. (45mm) high. Glue the inside and let dry.

3 Make a roll using six 3/16 x 11¾ in. (5 x 300mm) royal blue strips. Use your fingers to shape the roll into a cone 1 7/16 in. (35mm) high and with a slight curve at the tip. Glue the inside and let dry.

4 Make a roll using one 1/8 x 11¾ in. (3 x 300mm) royal blue strip. Use the tip of a paintbrush to shape it into a pointed and curved cone 7/16 in. (10mm) high. Glue the inside and let dry.

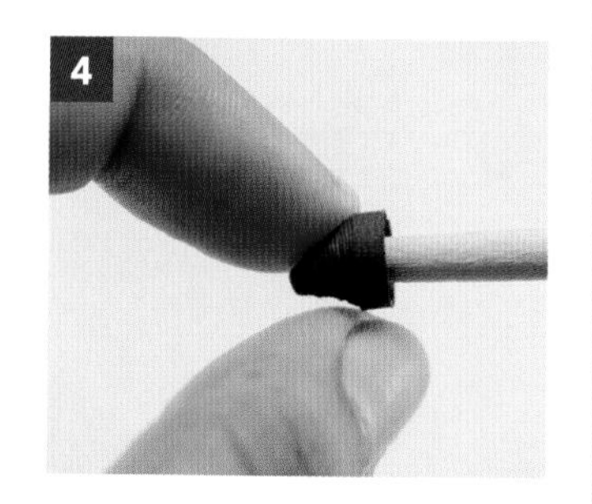

5 Make a roll using one 1/8 x 11¾ in. (3 x 300mm) royal blue strip. Use the tip of a paintbrush to shape it into a dome 3/16 in. (5mm) high. Glue the inside and let dry.

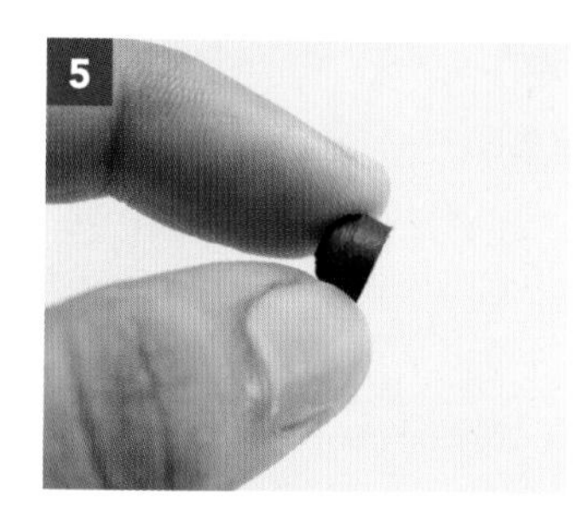

6 Glue the shapes made in steps 1 and 2 together, as shown in the photograph.

7 Glue the shape made in step 3 on to the upper curved part of the shape made in step 6. This will be the neck.

8 Glue the shapes made in steps 4 and 5 together to make the head and glue to the top of the neck.

Making the feathers

9 Join one 1/32 x 3 in. (1 x 75mm) royal blue strip to one 1/32 x 2 1/4 in. (1 x 55mm) light blue strip and quill into a roll (see Techniques page 121). Loosen the roll a little and glue in place. Press a needle tool into the center of the roll to create a depression.

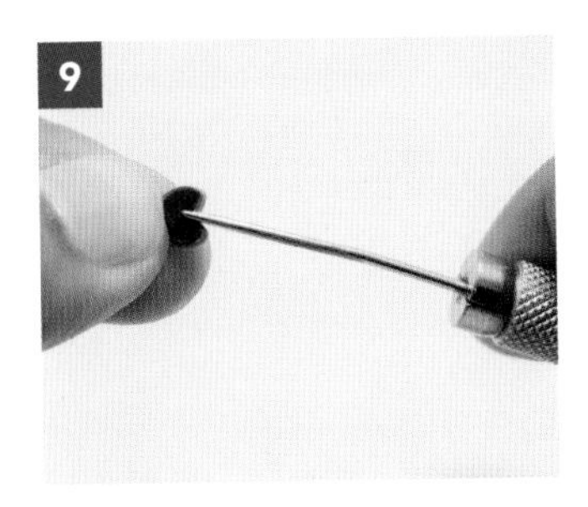

10 Quill a 1/32 x 3 3/4 in. (1 x 95mm) sea green strip around the shape made in step 9. Loosen it a little and press it on two sides at the top.

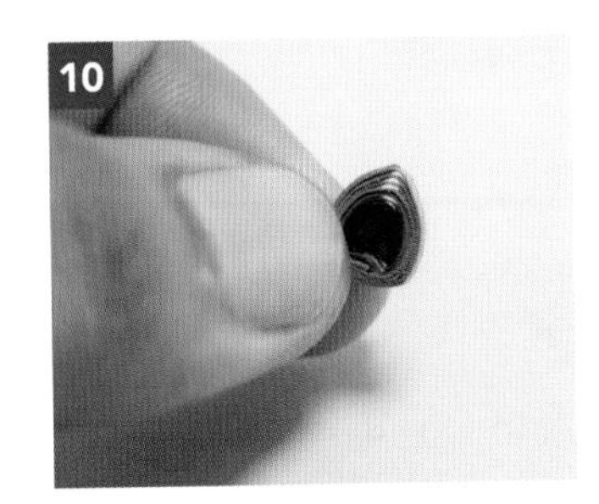

11 Join a 1/32 x 3 1/4 in. (1 x 85mm) green strip to a 1/32 x 2 1/2 in. (1 x 65mm) dark green strip. Quill it around the shape made in step 10 and glue the end in place. This shape will be the center of the feather. Make thirty-six similar centers. Set aside five of these shapes to use in step 26.

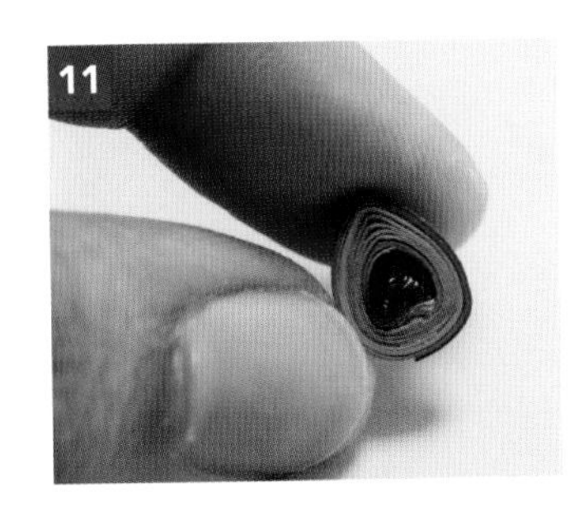

12 Stick a 1/32 x 1 3/4 in. (1 x 45mm) dark green strip around the center of the feather, leaving both ends protruding at the top.

13 Glue one 1/32 x 7/16 in. (1 x 10mm) dark green strip to one side of the feather so that the top is 1/16 in. (2mm) lower than the top of the previous one.

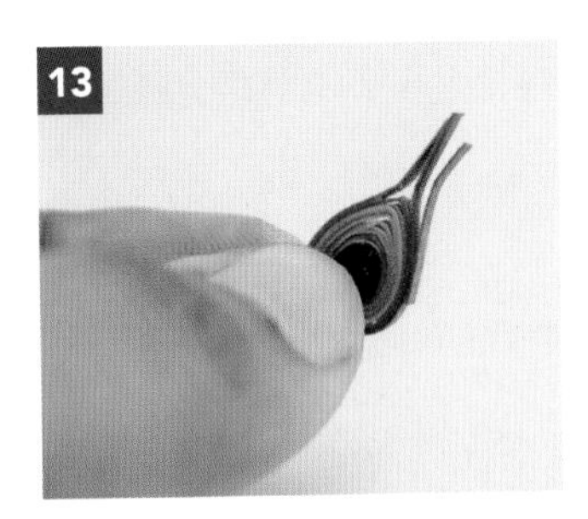

14 Glue three more 1/32 x 7/16 in. (1 x 10mm) dark green strips to the same side of the feather so that the top of each strip is 1/16–1/8 in. (2–3mm) lower than the previous one. The last strip should be glued to the center of the bottom of the feather.

15 Repeat steps 13 and 14 on the other side of the feather. Make a total of thirty-one feathers. Set aside five of these shapes to use in step 26.

16 Fold one 1/32 x 11 3/4 in. (1 x 300mm) dark green paper strip at a right angle 7/16 in. (10mm) from one end. Fold again in a zigzag manner and so that the next fold is 1/32 in. (1mm) lower than the previous fold.

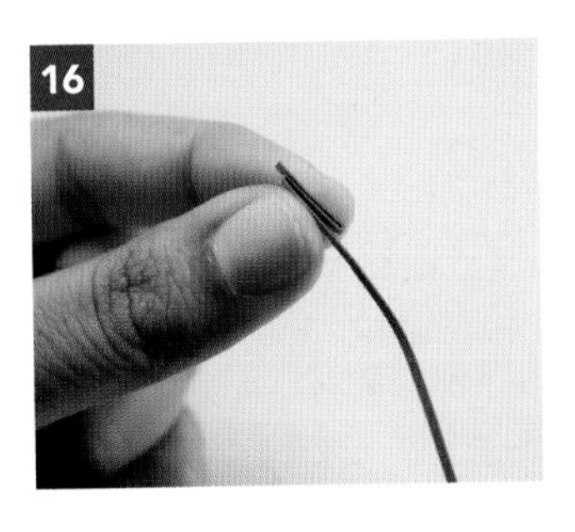

17 Continue to fold the strip in this way, then hold the folds together.

18 Apply glue to the folded edges and attach all the folds to one side of a 1/24 x 11¾ in. (1.5 x 300mm) strip of hard white paper.

19 Repeat steps 16 to 18 with one more strip and glue it to the other side of the white strip.

20 Use a thin, sharp pair of scissors to cut the joined folds to make each one a single strip.

21 Fan out the center. Repeat steps 16 to 21 to make twenty-six stemmed feathers.

22 Glue a feather center made in steps 9 to 15 to the top of each stemmed feather.

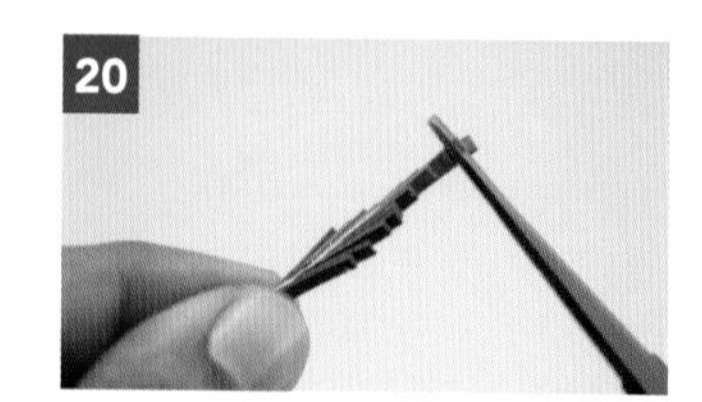

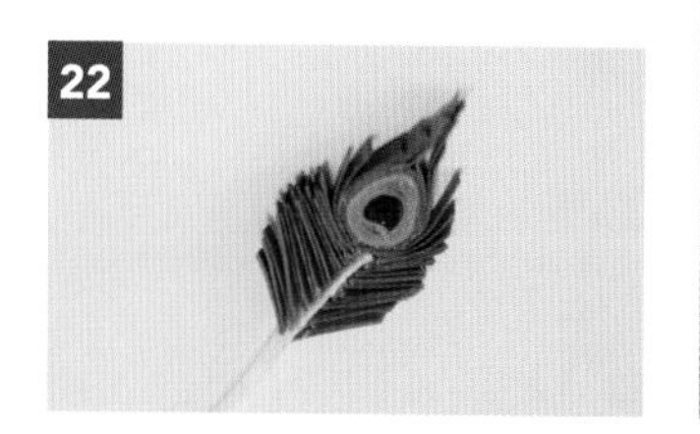

23 Glue the stems of six feathers together, keeping the feathers in a V-shape

24 Glue six more feathers below the previous six.

25 Continue to join sets of feathers, reducing the number of feathers for the next two rows to five feathers each, and the subsequent row to four feathers (only one row of four feathers).

26 Glue on the five feathers set aside in step 15, and then the five feathers set aside in step 11. Glue three feathers in a row.

27 Make five rolls, each one using one 1/32 x 3 in. (1 x 75mm) royal blue strip joined to one 1/32 x 2 1/4 in. (1 x 55mm) light blue strip, one 1/32 x 3 1/4 in. (1 x 85mm) green strip, and one 1/32 x 1 9/16 in. (1 x 40mm) dark green strip (see Techniques page 121). Make four rolls, each one using one 1/32 x 2 1/4 in. (1 x 55mm) light blue strip joined to one 1/32 x 3 1/4 in. (1 x 85mm) green strip, and one 1/32 x 1 9/16 in. (1 x 40mm) dark green strip. Make four rolls, each one using one 1/32 x 3 1/4 in. (1 x 85mm) green strip joined to one 1/32 x 1 9/16 in. (1 x 40mm) dark green strip. Make two rolls, each one using one 1/32 x 4 in. (1 x 100mm) turquoise strip. Loosen the rolls and glue from the backs.

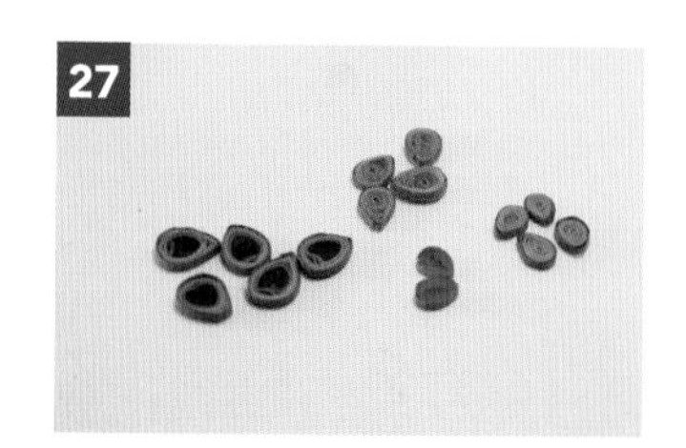

28 Glue the five rolls made in step 27 in the subsequent row of feathers.

29 Glue the other feathers at random in the next three rows. If necessary, trim the ends of the feathers so that the total strip is 3½ in. (9cm) long.

30 Glue the assembled feathers to the body to the point where the neck starts.

31 Use the circle punching machine to cut out forty circles from the turquoise and green paper sheets. Glue them to the body to cover the ends of the feathers and cover the body to the start of the neck. Arrange them so that they overlap and create a pattern similar to that shown in the photograph.

Making the wings

32 Using the templates on page 126, cut out the wing shapes from white paper. The photograph shows how they will be arranged when they have been decorated.

33 Cut a ⅛ x 11¾ in. (3 x 300mm) strip from the sheet of black paper. Glue it to a 3⁄16 x 11¾ in. (4 x 300mm) white strip so that the additional 1⁄32 in. (1mm) of white paper is visible on one long edge. Make as many strips as required.

34 Crimp the black and white strips in a zigzag by hand.

35 Cut the strips every two to three folds to make small sections. Take one section, stretch it a little but do not flatten it, then glue it white-side down to one of the wing shapes to create a three-dimensional effect. Glue on more pieces, overlapping them as you work up the wing shape.

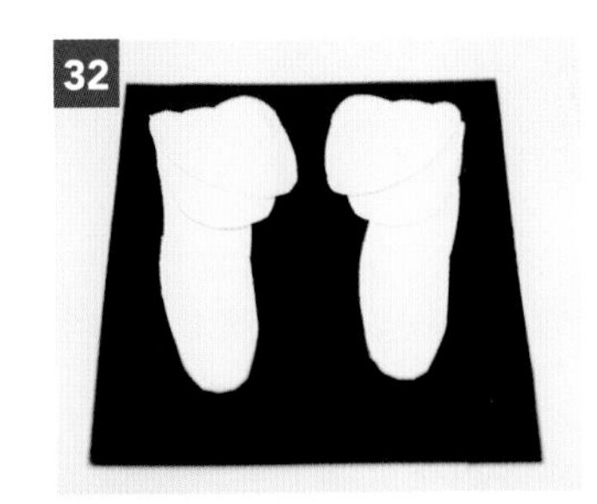

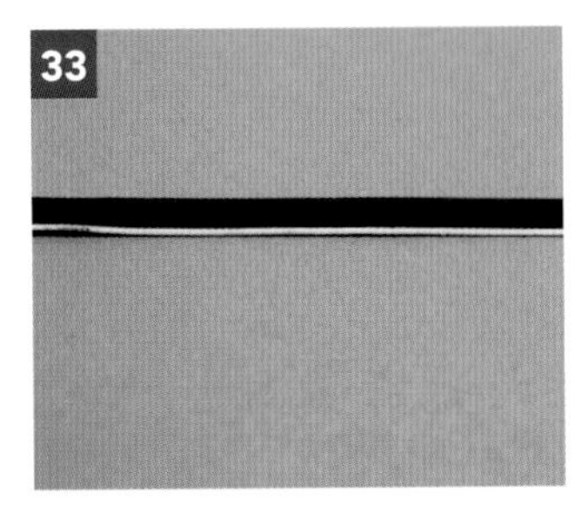

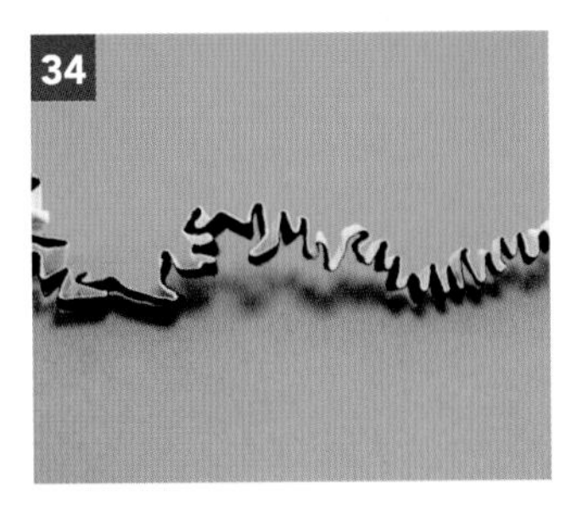

36 Fill all the wing sections in this way. Fold any protruding edges to the back of the wings and glue in place.

37 Glue the center wing sections to the bottom sections at an angle, as shown in the photograph. Glue the top pieces in the same way.

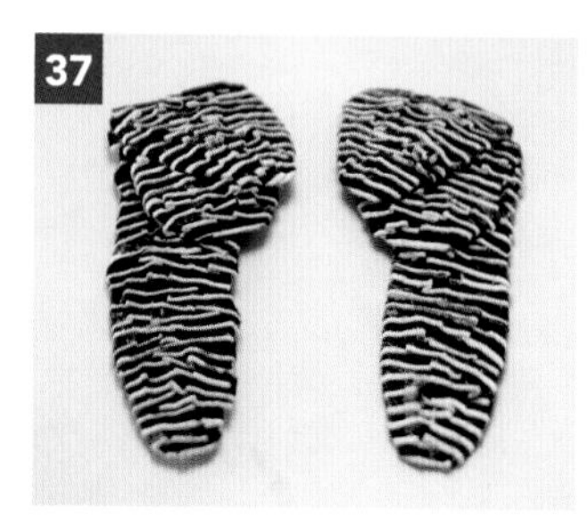

38 Glue one of the wings to each side of the body, with the broader ends at the neck.

Making the eyes and beak

39 Using the template on page 126 cut out the eyes from the sheets of white and black paper. Glue one eye to each side of the head.

40 Using the template on page 126 as a guide, cut a triangle from the sheet of white paper. On one base of the triangle mark a point $\frac{1}{16}$ in. (2mm) from one edge and from the tip to the base. The edge of the triangle should align with the center.

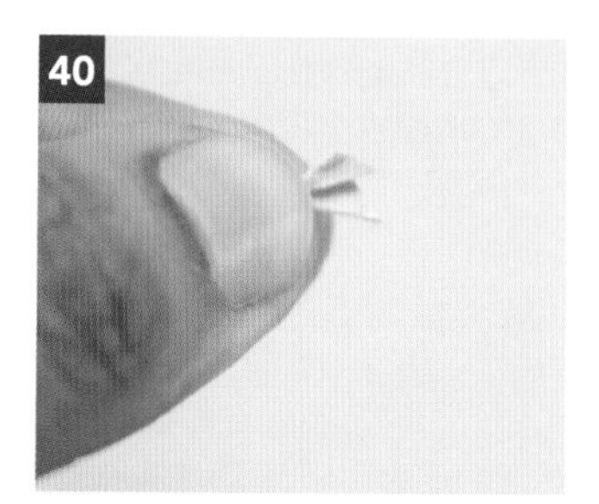

41 Fold the other side in the same way. Glue the folded sides together and trim the excess paper at the base.

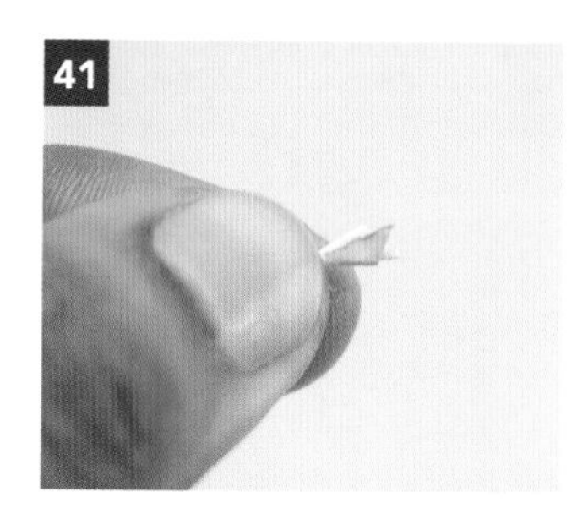

42 Press its sides using a slight pressure to give it a little volume. Glue the beak to the front of the head.

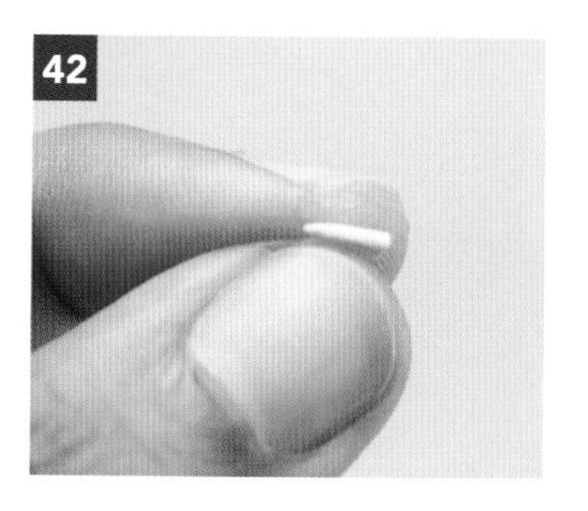

Making the crown

43 Quill one 1/24 x ¾ in. (1.5 x 20mm) strip of royal blue paper and make a roll. Glue this roll to the top of a 1/32 x 7/16 in. (1 x 10mm) strip of hard white paper. Make seven of these segments.

44 Glue the segments together at the base to make the crown.

45 Glue the crown to the head of the peacock.

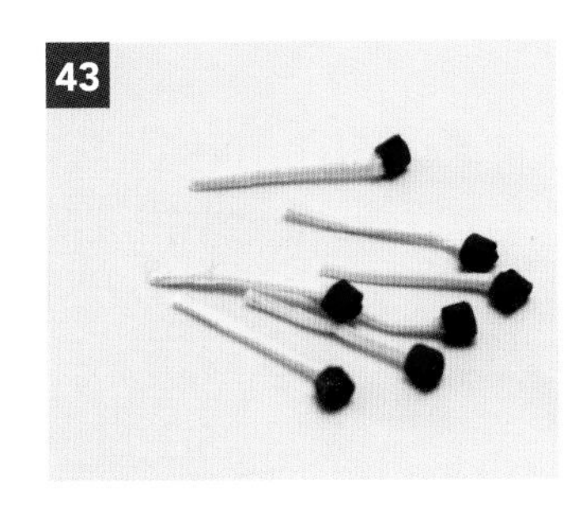

Making the legs

46 Quill one 3/16 x 4 in. (5 x 100mm) strip of cream paper on a quilling tool and make a cone 19/32 in. (15mm) long. Repeat to make a second cone. Glue from the inside and let dry.

47 Quill one 3/16 x 1 9/16 in. (5 x 40mm) cream strip and make a cone 7/16 in. (10mm) long. Make five more cones and glue the insides.

48 Glue three cones to the ends of a fourth cone to make one leg. Repeat to make a second leg. Apply a generous amount of glue and let dry completely.

49 Glue the legs to the body.

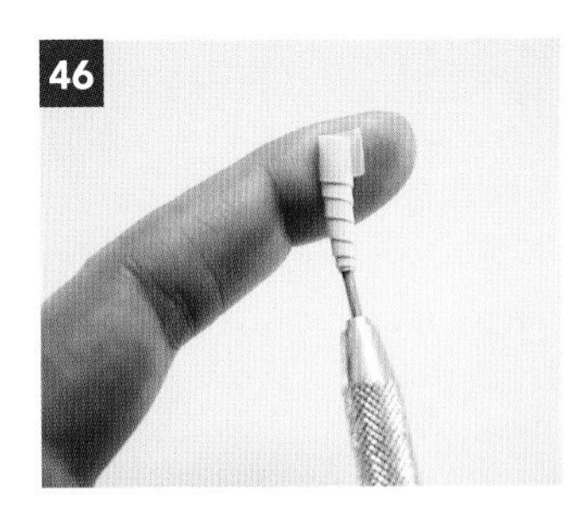

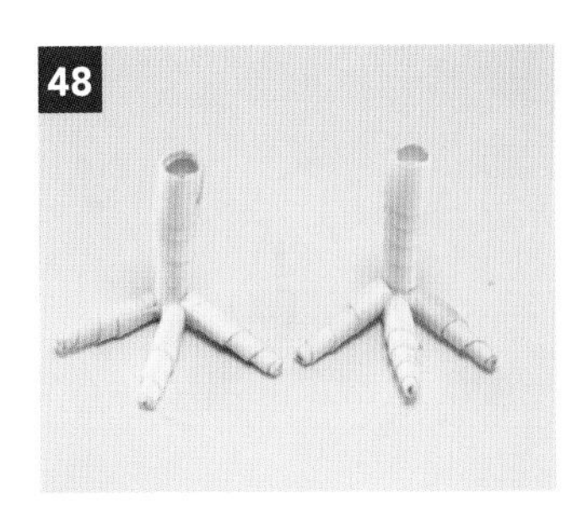

Animals

From the king of the jungle to the lowly tortoise, quilled paper rolls and cones are used to create a herd of creatures. When they are assembled, the paper coils bring each animal—a lion, monkey, elephant, and tortoise—to life.

Asian Elephant

Elephants are the largest of all land animals. They have a rich symbolism in Asia as they are closely associated with many religious and cultural traditions. Ganesha, one of the most popular gods in Indian mythology, is depicted with a human form and an elephant's head. There are two species of elephant: African and Asian. African elephants have larger ears than Asian ones.

Getting started

First cut all your strips using a steel ruler and paper cutter on a cutting mat (see Techniques page 120). The elephant has one body, one head, two ears, two tusks, four legs, and one tail.

- For the head and trunk you need thirty 3⁄16 x 11¾ in. (5 x 300mm) gray strips
- For the two ears you need thirty-two 1⁄24 x 11¾ in. (1.5 x 300mm) gray strips
- For the tusks you need two 3⁄16 x 4 in. (5 x 100mm) white strips
- For the body you need ninety-four 3⁄16 x 11¾ in. (5 x 300mm) and one 1⁄16 x 11¾ in. (2 x 300mm) gray strips
- For the legs you need twenty 3⁄16 x 11¾ in. (5 x 300mm) and forty-four 1⁄24 x 11¾ in. (1.5 x 300mm) gray strips
- For the tail you need one ¼ x 6 in. (7 x 150mm) gray strip and one 13⁄32 x 2 in. (10 x 50mm) black strip

You will need

Gray paper strips:
144 strips 3⁄16 x 11¾ in. (5 x 300mm)
76 strips 1⁄24 x 11¾ in. (1.5 x 300mm)
1 strip 1⁄16 x 11¾ in. (2 x 300mm)
1 strip ¼ x 6 in. (7 x 150mm)

White paper strips:
2 strips 3⁄16 x 4 in. (5 x 100mm)

Black paper strips:
1 strip 13⁄32 x 2 in. (10 x 50mm)

White, black, brown, and gray paper sheets:
1 A4-size sheet of each color

Steel ruler
Paper cutter
Cutting mat
Quilling tool
Mini Mold
Glue
Paintbrush
Quilling comb
Needle tool
Sharp pair of scissors
Paper knife

Finished size

Approximately 3½ in. (9cm) long

Difficulty level

Advanced

Making the head and trunk

1 Make a roll using fifteen 3/16 x 11¾ in. (5 x 300mm) gray paper strips (see Techniques page 121). Shape it into a dome and glue from the inside (see Techniques page 125).

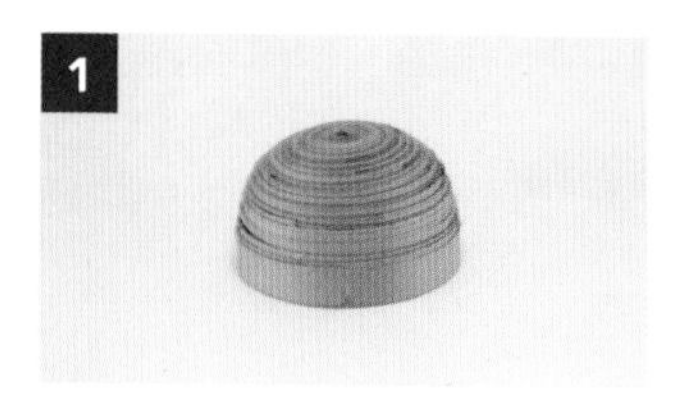

2 Make a second roll using fifteen 3/16 x 11¾ in. (5 x 300mm) gray paper strips. Shape it into a dome as before and then use your fingers to elongate the dome. Use the tip of a paintbrush to extend the narrow end.

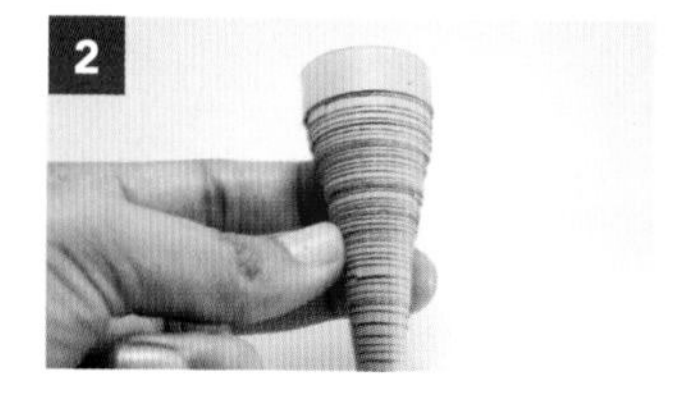

3 Press the narrow tip from the back to create a curve. Glue the trunk from the inside and let dry.

4 Glue the dome to the trunk to make the head.

Making the ears

5 Make a loose roll using ten 1/24 x 11¾ in. (1.5 x 300mm) gray paper strips.

6 Press the roll from two opposite points on one side to make an ear shape. Repeat steps 5 and 6 to make a second ear and flip it horizontally so that it is a mirror image of the first ear.

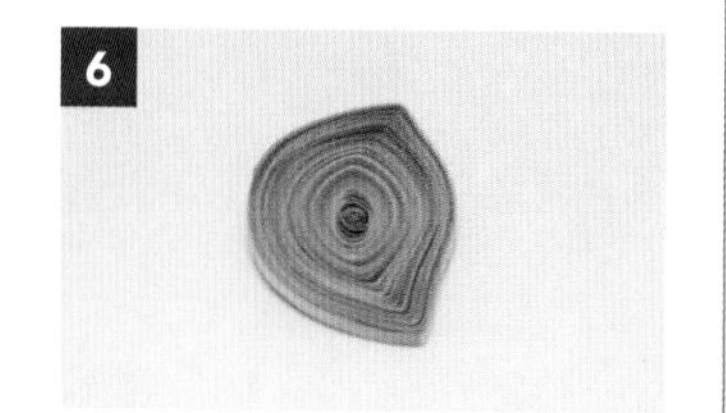

7 Carefully press the coils to give a little depth to both ears.

8 Use one 1/24 x 11¾ in. (1.5 x 300mm) gray paper strip to make an O-shape (see Techniques page 124). Repeat to make five more O-shapes (three for each ear).

9 Fold the O-shapes in half and open them out. Glue one O-shape at the upper pointed edge of the ear, attaching both sides of the O-shape to the opposite sides of the pointed tip of the ear.

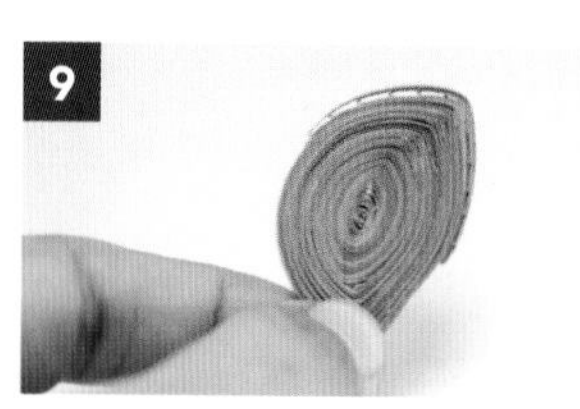

10 Wrap one 1/24 x 11¾ in. (1.5 x 300mm) gray paper strip around the perimeter of the ear.

11 Repeat steps 9 and 10 with the remaining two O-shapes to make the ear larger. Repeat steps 8 to 11 for the second ear.

12 Glue one ear to each side of the head.

Making the tusks

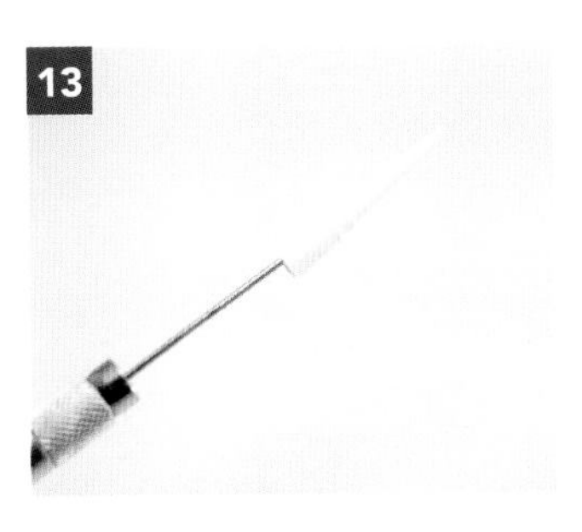

13 Quill one 3⁄16 x 4 in. (5 x 100mm) white paper strip. Use a needle tool to push the roll outward into a narrow cone shape. Glue it from the inside. Repeat to make a second tusk.

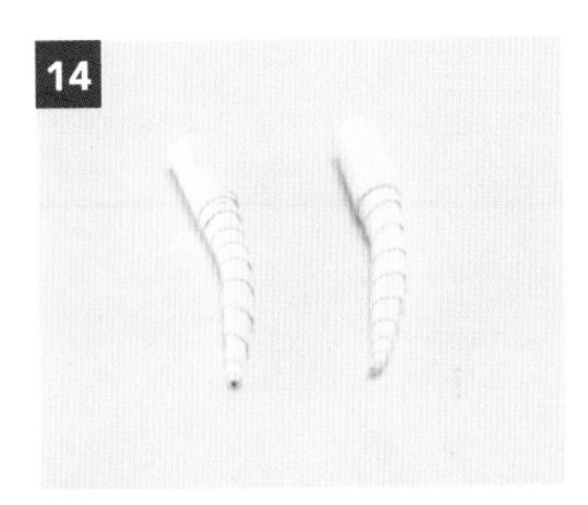

14 Push the cones backward to make a curved shape. Glue them from the inside and press the wide ends of the tusks flat. Let dry.

15 Cut two semicircles of gray paper 7⁄16 in. (10mm) in diameter. Glue the semicircles to the top of the tusks so that they cover the flattened sections. Fold any excess paper to the back of the tusks.

16 Glue the tusks to the head, one on each side of the trunk.

Making the body

17 Make a roll using thirty 3⁄16 x 11¾ in. (5 x 300mm) gray paper strips. Shape it into a dome using a Mini Mold (see Techniques page 125). Push the center to make a pointed shape, then slowly push the lower sides of the dome upward to make a broad, heightened dome. Do not push the dome so much that the coils start to open up. The finished dome should be about 13⁄16 in. (30mm) high. Apply glue to the inside and let dry.

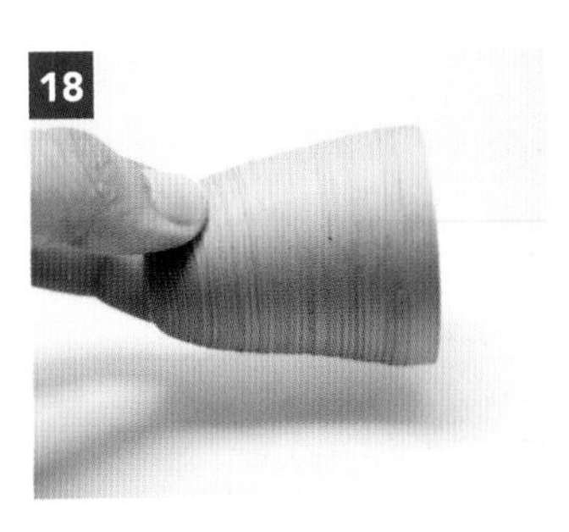

18 Make a second roll using thirty 3⁄16 x 11¾ in. (5 x 300mm) gray paper strips. Shape it into a dome using a Mini Mold. Push the center to make a pointed shape, then slowly push the sides of the dome upward to make a narrow, heightened dome. Do not push the dome so much that the coils start to open up. The finished dome should be about 2 in. (50mm) high. Apply glue to the inside and let dry.

19 Position the domes so that the base of the narrow dome sits inside the base of the broad dome at an angle and with a gap at the base as shown in the photograph. Glue them together and let dry.

20 Make a third roll using thirty-two 3⁄16 x 11¾ in. (5 x 300mm) gray paper strips. Press it into a dome. Glue it from the inside and let dry. Glue the dome between the gap in the shape made in step 19. Flip the body vertically, ready for the next step.

21 Glue the head to the flat front section of the body.

22 To fill the gap between the face and the body, apply glue to one side of two 3⁄16 x 11¾ in. (5 x 300mm) gray strips and one 1⁄16 x 11¾ in. (2 x 300mm) gray strip. Wrap the wider strips around the gap, followed by the narrow strip, to hide the join.

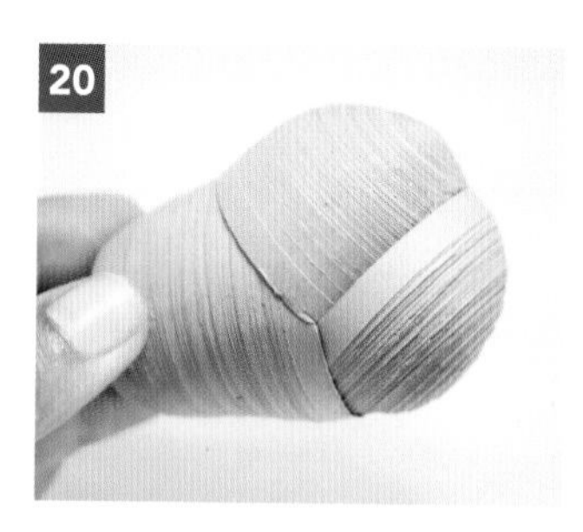

Making the legs

23 Quill five 3⁄16 x 11¾ in. (5 x 300mm) gray strips into a roll. Use a finger to push the roll outward until it is 2 in. (50mm) long. Repeat to make a total of four legs.

24 Press the narrow ends of the legs on the Mini Mold to shape them into a concave dome. Shape the legs until they are slightly curved. Glue from the inside and let dry.

25 Make a roll using seven 1⁄24 x 11¾ in. (1.5 x 300mm) gray strips. Repeat to make four rolls. Shape the rolls into domes. Glue the domes from the inside and let dry. Glue one dome inside the wide end of each leg. Cut a 1-in. (25mm) slit in the center-back of each leg and overlap the cut edges to flatten the back so that it will sit against the elephant's body.

26 Glue two legs to each side of the body, making sure the elephant is level when it stands. Let dry.

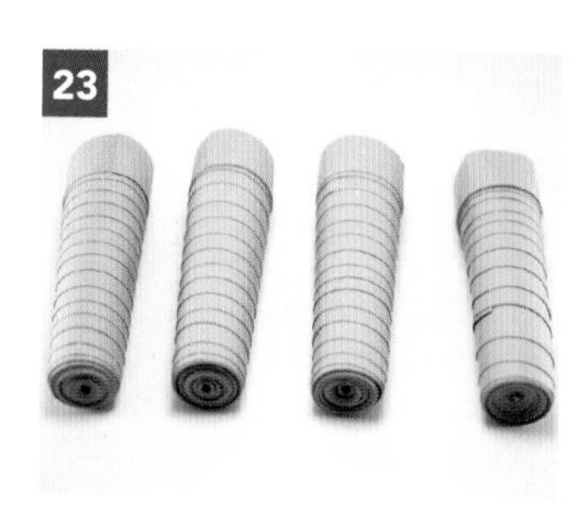

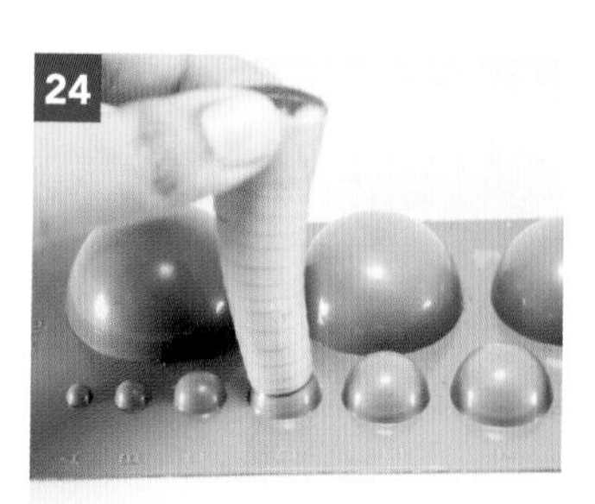

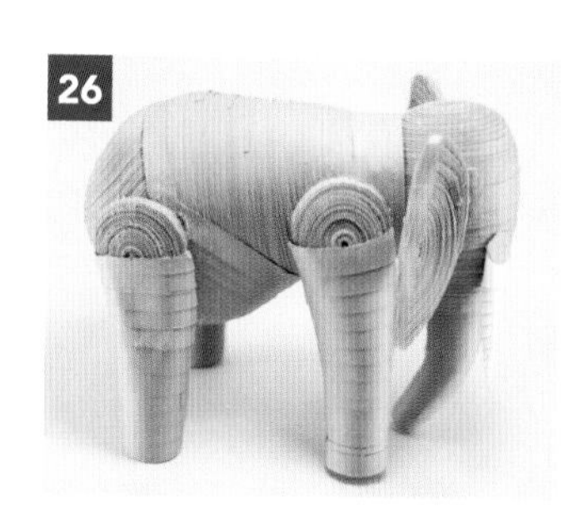

Making the feet

27 Make a roll using four 1⁄24 x 11¾ in. (1.5 x 300mm) gray strips. Repeat to make four rolls. Use a Mini Mold to shape the rolls into domes. Glue the domes from the inside and let dry. Glue one dome to the base of each leg and let dry.

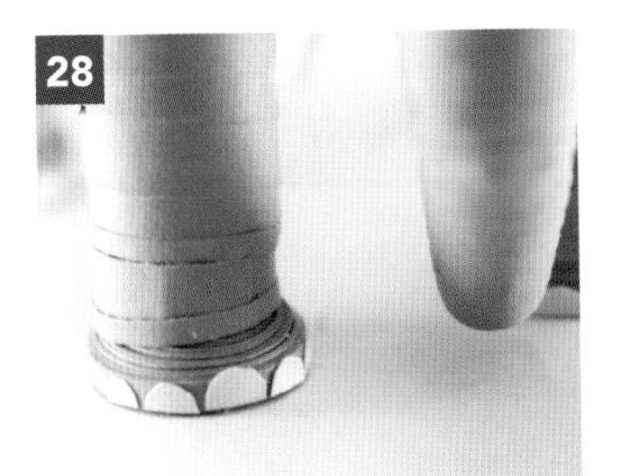

28 Use a paper knife to cut twenty semicircles ⅛ in. (4mm) in diameter from the sheet of white paper. Glue five semicircles to the front of each foot to make the nails.

Making the eyes and tail

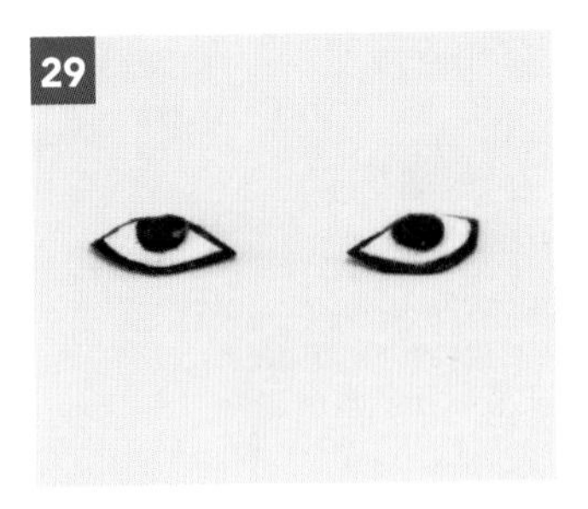

29 Cut two tapered ovals from the sheet of black paper. Cut two smaller tapered ovals from the sheet of white paper and glue to the black shapes. Cut two small disks from the sheet of brown paper and glue in place to complete the eyes. Glue the eyes to the elephant's face, a short distance above the tusks.

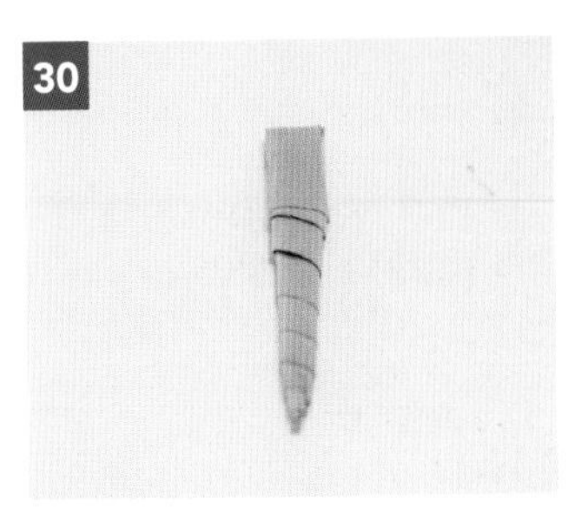

30 Make a roll from one ¼ x 6 in. (7 x 150mm) gray strip. Use a needle tool to shape it into a narrow cone. Glue it from the inside and press it flat. Let dry.

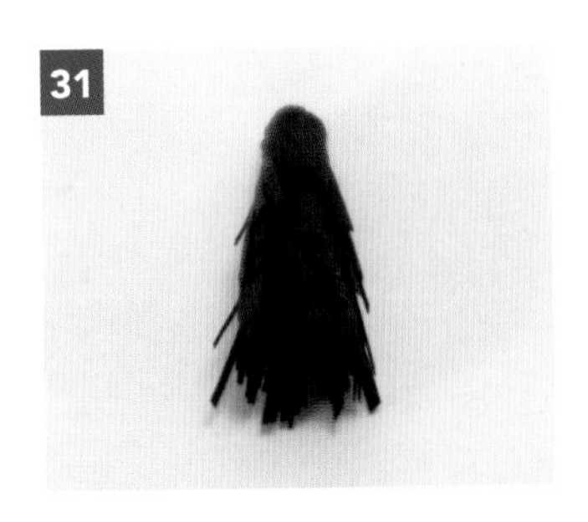

31 Use a pair of scissors to cut a fringe along one long edge of one 13⁄32 x 2 in. (10 x 50mm) black strip. Quill the uncut edge of the strip and glue its base.

32 Glue the fringed black tail hair to the tip of the flattened cone. Glue the tail to the back of the elephant's body. Let dry.

African Lion

In the Bible, the male lion represents strength, leadership, and predatory ferocity, and so it is perhaps no wonder that it is often called the "king" of the jungle. Famed for the adult male's long mane, the lion is the largest of Africa's big cats and lives in social groups, unlike other big cats that prefer to live alone. A group of lions, called a pride, may consist of fifteen to twenty lions, with up to three males.

Getting started

First cut all your strips using a steel ruler and paper cutter on a cutting mat (see Techniques page 120). The lion has one head, one body, one snout, two ears, four legs, and one tail.

- For the face you need nineteen ⅛ x 11¾ in. (3 x 300mm) ocher strips
- For the body you need eighty 3/16 x 11¾ in. (5 x 300mm) ocher strips
- For the ears you need three 1/32 x 11¾ in. (1 x 300mm) ocher strips
- For the legs you need seven 1/24 x 11¾ in. (1.5 x 300mm) and ten ¼ x 11¾ in. (7 x 300mm) ocher strips
- For the feet you need four ⅛ x 10¼ in. (3 x 260 mm) and sixteen 1/32 x 2 19/32 in. (1 x 60mm) ocher strips
- For the snout you need one 1/32 x 13¾ in. (1 x 350mm) and two 1/32 x 9¾ in. (1 x 250mm) white strips and one 1/32 x 6 in. (1 x 150mm) dark brown strip
- For the mane you need thirty-five 3/16 x 1 9/16 in. (5 x 40mm), twenty 3/16 x 2¾ in. (5 x 70mm), twenty 3/16 x 4 5/16 in. (5 x 110mm), and eighty 3/16 x 5½ in. (5 x 140mm) dark brown strips
- For the tail you need one ¼ x 7¾ in. (7 x 200mm) ocher strip and one 13/32 x 2 in. (10 x 50mm) black strip
- For the eyes and whiskers you need A4 sheets of white, black, ocher, and brown paper

You will need

Ocher paper strips:
19 strips ⅛ x 11¾ in. (3 x 300mm)
80 strips 3/16 x 11¾ in. (5 x 300mm)
3 strips 1/32 x 11¾ in. (1 x 300mm)
7 strips 1/24 x 11¾ in. (1.5 x 300mm)
10 strips ¼ x 11¾ in. (7 x 300mm)
4 strips ⅛ x 10¼ (3 x 260 mm)
16 strips 1/32 x 2 19/32 in. (1 x 60mm)
1 strip ¼ x 7¾ in. (7 x 200mm)

White paper strips:
1 strip 1/32 x 13¾ in. (1 x 350mm)
2 strips 1/32 x 9¾ in. (1 x 250mm)

Dark brown paper strips:
1 strip 1/32 x 6 in. (1 x 150mm)
35 strips 3/16 x 1 9/16 in. (5 x 40mm)
20 strips 3/16 x 2¾ in. (5 x 70mm)
20 strips 3/16 x 4 5/16 in. (5 x 110mm)
80 strips 3/16 x 5½ in. (5 x 140mm)

Black paper strips:
1 strip 13/32 x 2 in. (10 x 50mm)

White, black, ocher, and brown paper:
1 A4-size sheet of each color

Steel ruler
Paper cutter
Cutting mat
Quilling tool
Mini Mold
Glue
Paintbrush
Needle tool
Sharp pair of scissors
Paper knife

Finished size

Approximately 6¼ in. (160mm) long

Difficulty level

Advanced

Making the body

1 Make a roll using nineteen 3/16 x 11¾ in. (5 x 300mm) ocher strips (see Techniques page 121). Use your fingers to extend it into a dome 1 9/16 in. (40mm) tall and slightly narrower at the top than at the base. Make a second roll using thirty 3/16 x 11¾ in. (5 x 300mm) ocher strips. Use your fingers to extend it into a dome 2 in. (5mm) tall. Glue from the inside and let dry.

2 Glue the closed end of the larger dome inside the open end of the smaller dome.

3 Make a roll using thirty-one 3/16 x 11¾ in. (5 x 300mm) ocher strips. Use your fingers to extend it slightly into a dome 7/16 in. (10mm) tall and press it flat from the top. Glue from the inside and let dry.

4 Glue the dome onto the open end of the shape made in step 2. The combined shape should be about 3⅛ in. (80mm) long.

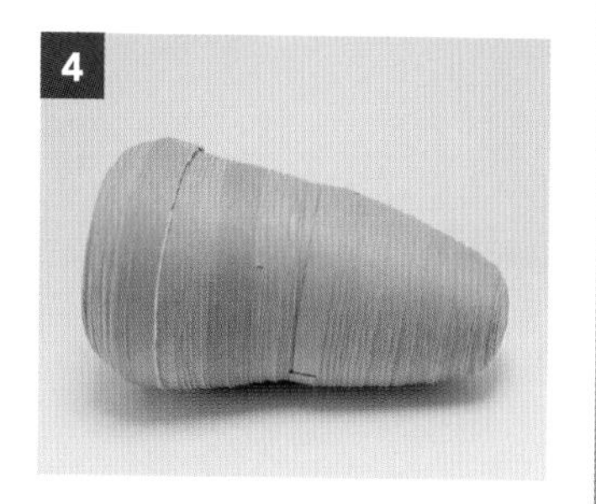

Making the head

5 Make a roll using nine 1/8 x 11¾ in. (3 x 300mm) ocher strips. Use a Mini Mold to make it into a dome 1 3/16 in. (30mm) high (see Techniques page 125). Use your fingers to extend the dome so the tip is considerably narrower than the base and there is a depression in the middle. Make a second dome using ten 1/8 x 11¾ in. (3 x 300mm) ocher strips. Use your fingers to extend it into a dome 7/16 in. (10mm) tall and press it flat from the top. Glue both the domes from the inside and let dry.

6 Glue the open ends of the domes together to make the head.

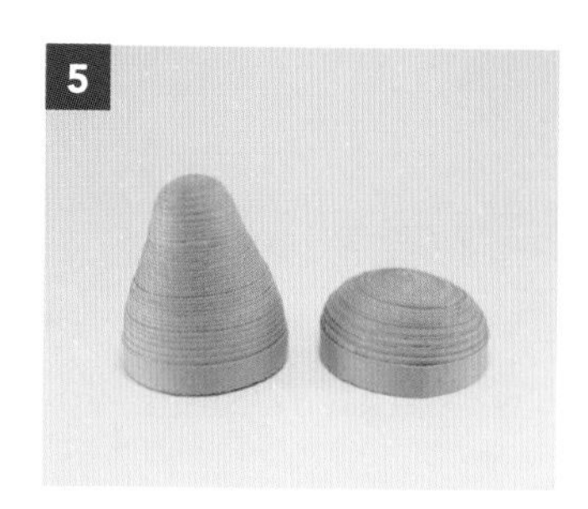

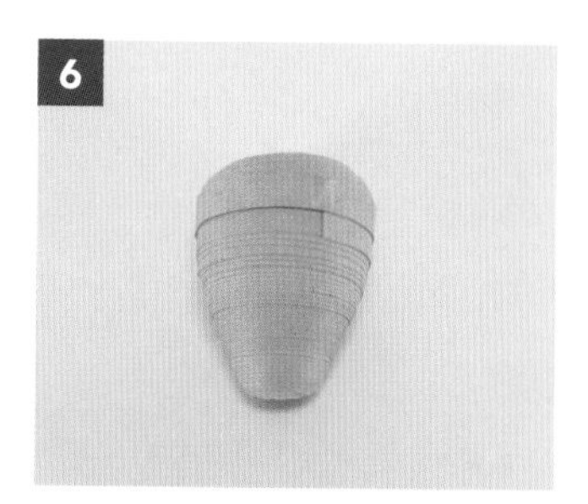

Making the snout and nose

7 Make a roll using one 1/32 x 9¾ in. (1 x 250mm) white strip. Loosen it (see Techniques page 122) then pinch the top and shape it as shown in the photograph. Glue from the back and let dry. Repeat to make a second roll and shape it so that it is a mirror image of the first roll.

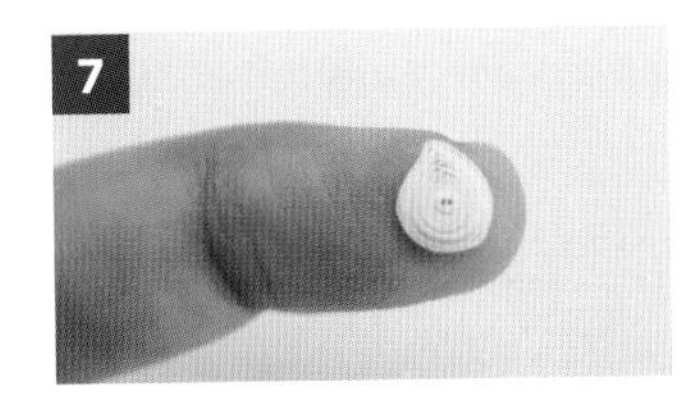

8 Make a roll using one 1/32 x 13¾ in. (1 x 350mm) white strip. Loosen the roll and glue the end in place. Shape it into a semicircle by pressing the roll from two sides, then shape it into a dome. Use your fingers to give the semicircle some depth like a dome. Glue from the back and let dry.

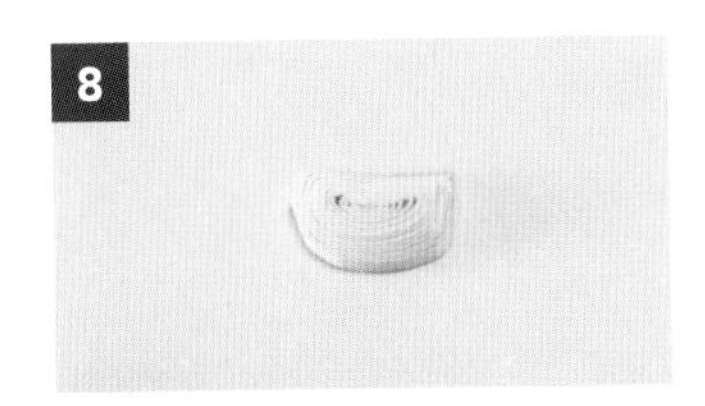

9 Make a roll using one 1/32 x 6 in. (1 x 150mm) dark brown strip and loosen it.

10 Press the roll from three sides to make a triangle. Press the center against a needle tool to create a slight depression.

11 Glue the shape made in step 8 to the narrow section of the head as shown in the photograph.

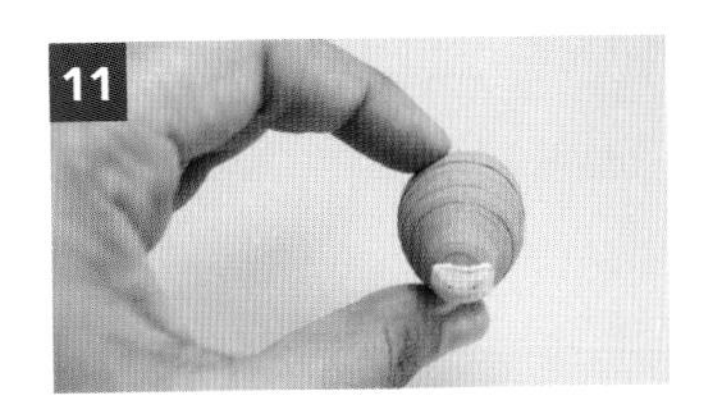

12 Glue the shapes made in step 7 so that they overlap the first shape and the pinched points face each other. Glue the nose between them.

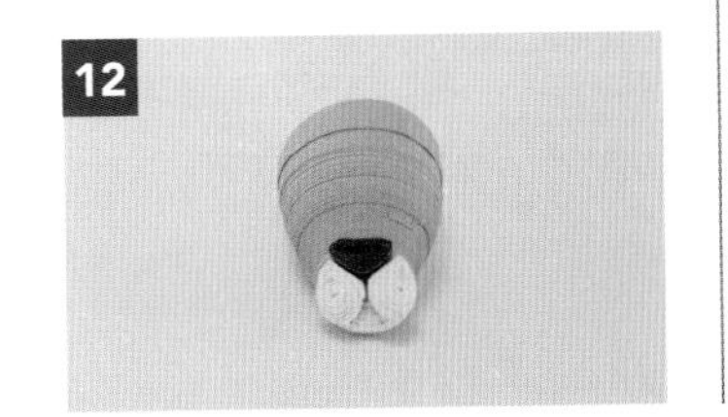

Making the ears and eyes

13 Make a roll using one-and-a-half 1/32 x 11¾ in. (1 x 300mm) ocher strips and loosen it. Press the roll from the base and sides to create the shape shown in the photograph. Glue the back. Repeat to make a second shape. Glue one ear to each side of the head.

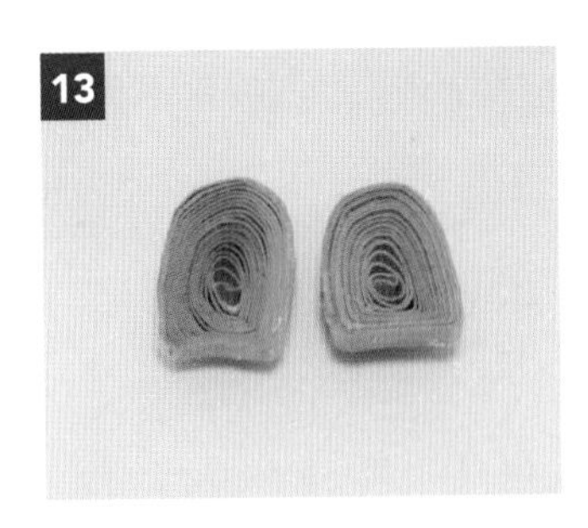

14 Cut two tapered ovals from the sheet of white paper. Cut two smaller tapered ovals from the sheet of dark brown paper and glue to the white shapes. Cut two small disks from the sheet of ocher paper and glue in place. Cut two small disks from the sheet of dark brown paper and glue in place. Cut two small dots of white paper and glue in place to complete the eyes.

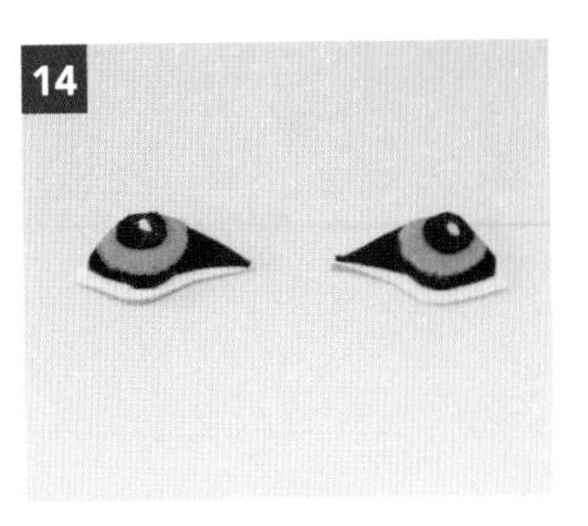

15 Glue the eyes to the face. Cut eight or ten very thin strips of white paper and glue to each side of the snout to represent whiskers.

16 Glue the head to the top of the broad side of the body.

Making the mane

17 To make the mane you need four lengths of cones. The number of cones required depends on the desired thickness of the mane. The lion shown here required thirty-five 3/16 x 1 9/16 in. (5 x 40mm) cones, twenty 3/16 x 2 3/4 in. (5 x 70mm) cones, twenty 3/16 x 4 5/16 in. (5 x 110mm) cones, and eighty 3/16 x 5 1/2 in. (5 x 140mm) cones. Make the cones by quilling on the quilling tool itself, or by making a roll and extending it using a needle tool (see Techniques page 121). Extend the 3/16 x 1 9/16 in. (5 x 40mm) cones to 7/16 in. (10mm), the 3/16 x 2 3/4 in. (5 x 70mm) cones to 19/32 in. (15mm), the 3/16 x 4 5/16 in. (5 x 110mm) cones to 3/4 in. (20mm), and the 3/16 x 5 1/2 in. (5 x 140mm) cones to 1 9/16 in. (40mm). Glue the cones from the inside, then press them flat.

18 Glue the 1 9/16 in. (40mm) cones at the front of the neck, then start to add them to the sides of the neck.

19 Glue more 1 9/16 in. (40mm) cones at the back of the neck. Keep adding layers to get more volume around the face, gluing one layer on top of another and working up the back of the head.

20 As you reach the middle of the head, start to add the 3/4 in. (20mm) cones around the head and face.

21 When you get to the front of the head, start to use the 19/32 in. (15mm) cones. The mane should sit on the back of the head as shown in the photograph.

22 Finally glue the 7/16 in. (10mm) cones at the front of the head. Let the glue dry completely, then adjust the shape of the cones to shape the mane.

Making the legs and tail

23 Make a roll using two-and-a-half ¼ x 11¾ in. (7 x 300mm) ocher strips. Use your fingers to extend the roll to 1⅜ in. (30mm) long. Press one side of each cone flat to make the base. Glue the inside and let dry. Repeat to make a second roll.

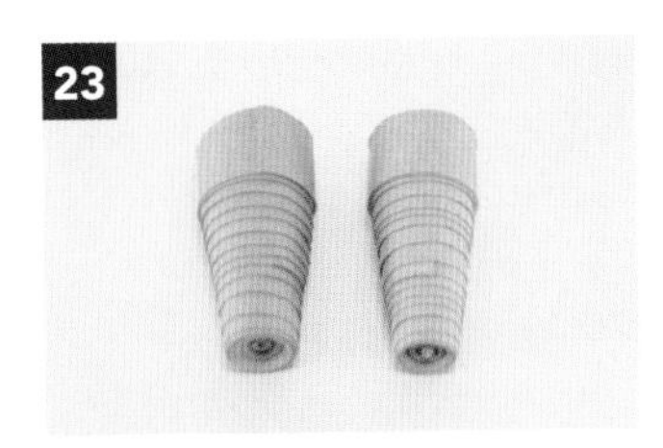

24 Glue the cones to the front of the body.

25 Make a roll using two-and-a-half ¼ x 11¾ in. (7 x 300mm) ocher strips. Use your fingers to extend the roll to 1 7/16 in. (35mm) long. Press one side flat to make the base. Glue the inside and let dry. Repeat to make a second cone.

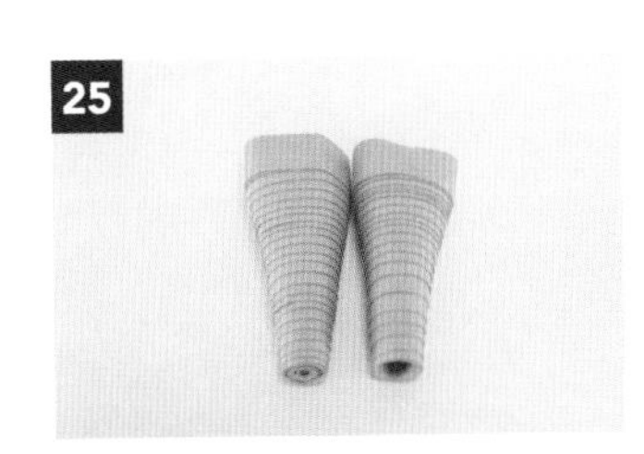

26 Make a dome using seven 1/24 x 11¾ in. (1.5 x 300mm) ocher strips. Glue the dome inside the wider end of one of the rolls made in step 25. Make a ¾in. (20mm) cut at the center-back of this roll. Cut a semicircle from the back of the other roll made in step 25.

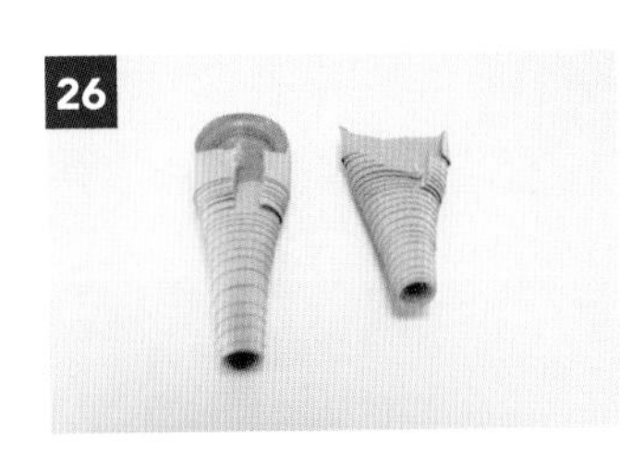

27 Quill one ⅛ x 10¼ in. (3 x 260 mm) ocher strip. Quill straight for 6 in. (150mm) to make a roll, then tilt the strip to extend the roll into a cone. Repeat to make a total of four cones. Glue from the inside and let dry.

28 Quill one 1/32 x 2 19/32 in. (1 x 60mm) ocher strip into a roll and loosen it. Press from two sides then flatten it into a semicircle. Repeat to make a total of sixteen semicircles.

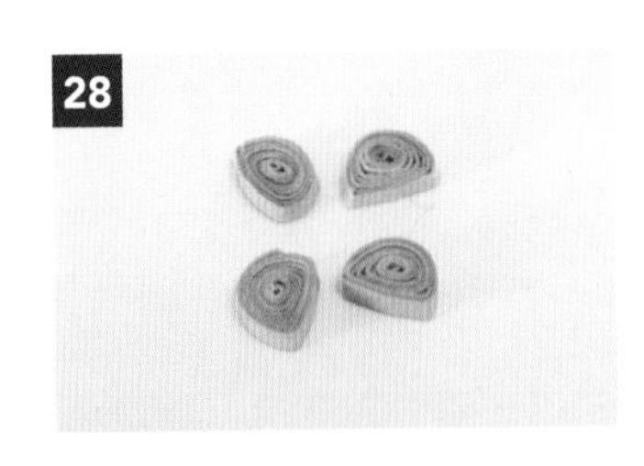

29 Glue four semicircles to the inside-front of the wide end of each foot.

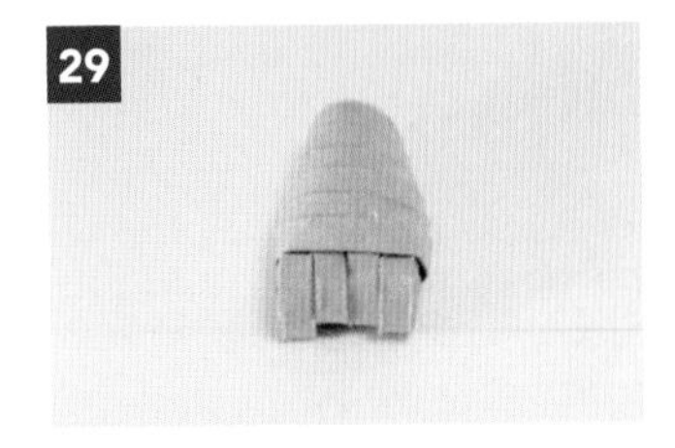

30 Use a quilling tool to make a cone using one ¼ x 7¾ in. (7 x 200mm) ocher strip. The cone should be 2 in. (50mm) long. Glue the inside and press flat. Take one 13/32 x 2 in. (10 x 50mm) black strip and use a pair of scissors to cut a fringe along one long edge. Quill the strip and glue it to the tip of the cone shape to complete the tail.

31 Glue two feet to the front legs. Glue the leg without the dome below the lion's body, with the cut side of the leg facing downward.

32 Glue the leg with the dome to the upper back section of the body. Glue the remaining feet to the rear legs. Glue the tail to the back of the lion.

Monkey

Monkeys are intelligent, social animals. They can be distinguished from apes by their tails and narrow chests. In the Chinese zodiac, the monkey represents versatility, movement, and activity. If you are born in the year of the monkey, it is said that you are quick-witted, and a fast thinker. The Hindu god Hanuman is a monkey and is worshipped as a divine protector and an embodiment of strength.

Getting started

First cut all your strips using a steel ruler and paper cutter on a cutting mat (see Techniques page 120). The monkey has one body, one head, two ears, two legs, two arms, and one tail.

- For the body you need forty-one 3/16 x 11¾ in. (5 x 300mm) brown strips
- For the head you need nineteen ⅛ x 11¾ in. (3 x 300mm) and two 1/32 x 11¾ in. (1 x 300mm) brown strips; eight 1/32 x 11¾ in. (1 x 300mm) light brown strips; and sheets of black and white paper
- For the legs you need eight 3/16 x 11¾ in. (5 x 300mm), five ⅛ x 11¾ in. (3 x 300mm), two 3/16 x 7¾ in. (5 x 200mm), and ten ⅛ x 1 3/16 in. (3 x 30 mm) brown strips
- For the arms you need six 3/16 x 11¾ in. (5 x 300mm), three ⅛ x 11¾ in. (3 x 300mm), two 3/16 x 6 in. (5 x 150mm), and ten ⅛ x 1 3/16 in. (3 x 30 mm) brown strips
- For the tail you need one ¼ x 7¾ in. (7 x 200mm) brown strip

You will need

Brown paper strips:
55 strips 3/16 x 11¾ in. (5 x 300mm)
27 strips ⅛ x 11¾ in. (3 x 300mm)
2 strips 1/32 x 11¾ in. (1 x 300mm)
2 strips 3/16 x 7¾ in. (5 x 200mm)
20 strips ⅛ x 1 3/16 in. (3 x 30 mm)
2 strips 3/16 x 6 in. (5 x 150mm)
1 strip ¼ x 7¾ in. (7 x 200mm)

Light brown paper strips:
8 strips 1/32 x 11¾ in. (1 x 300mm)

White and black paper:
1 A4 sheet of each color

Steel ruler
Paper cutter
Cutting mat
Quilling tool
Mini Mold
Glue
Paintbrush
Sharp pair of scissors
Needle tool
Paper knife

Finished size

Approximately 3⅛ in. (8cm) high

Difficulty level

Moderate

Making the body

1 Make a roll using twenty ³⁄₁₆ x 11¾ in. (5 x 300mm) brown strips (see Techniques page 121). Use your fingers to extend it into a dome about 1⁷⁄₁₆ in. (35mm) high. Glue the inside and let dry.

2 Make a roll using twenty-one ³⁄₁₆ x 11¾ in. (5 x 300mm) brown strips. Use your fingers to extend it into a dome about 1 in. (25mm) high. The tip should be broader than the top of the dome made in step 1. Glue the inside and let dry.

3 Glue the open ends of the domes together, with the dome made in step 1 uppermost.

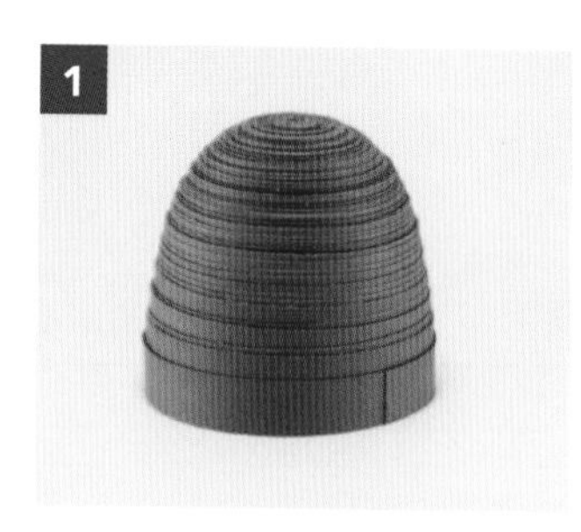
1

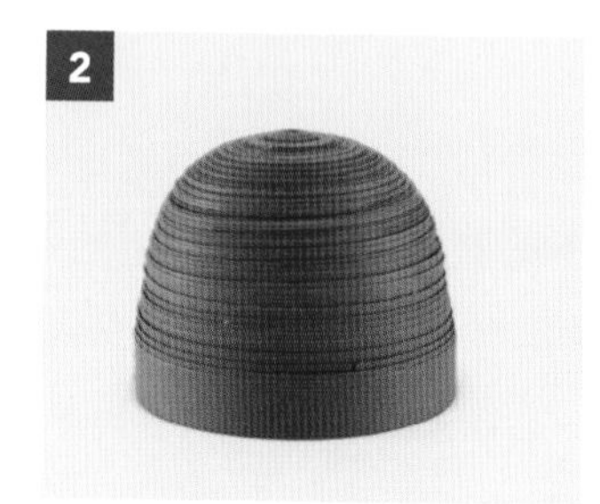
2

3

Making the head

4 Make a roll using nine ⅛ x 11¾ in. (3 x 300mm) brown strips. Use your fingers to extend it into a dome about ¾ in. (20mm) high. Glue the inside and let dry.

5 Make a roll using ten ⅛ x 11¾ in. (3 x 300mm) brown strips. Use your fingers to extend it into a dome about ⁷⁄₁₆ in. (10mm) high. Glue the inside and let dry.

6 Glue the open ends of the domes made in steps 4 and 5 together to make the head.

7 Make a roll using three ¹⁄₃₂ x 11¾ in. (1 x 300mm) light brown strips. Shape it in a dome (see Techniques page 125). Repeat to make a second dome. Glue the domes from the inside and let dry.

8 When the domes are dry, cut off one-third of each one and discard the smaller sections.

9 Glue the two dome sections together from the back, leaving a gap between them in the front, to make the mouth as shown in the photograph.

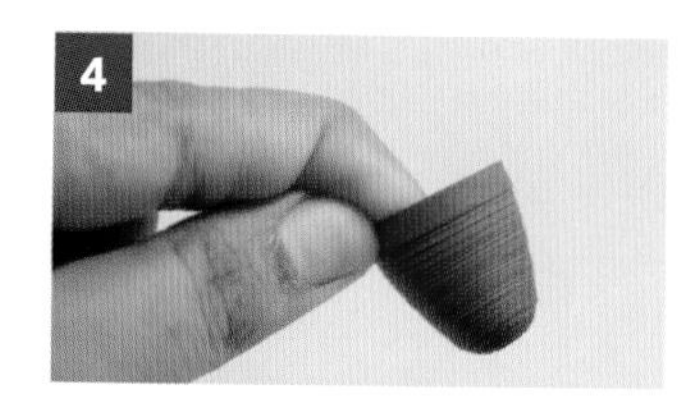
4

5

6

7

8

9

10 Make a roll using one 1⁄32 x 11¾ in. (1 x 300mm) light brown strip. Repeat to make a second roll in the same way. These will be the eyes.

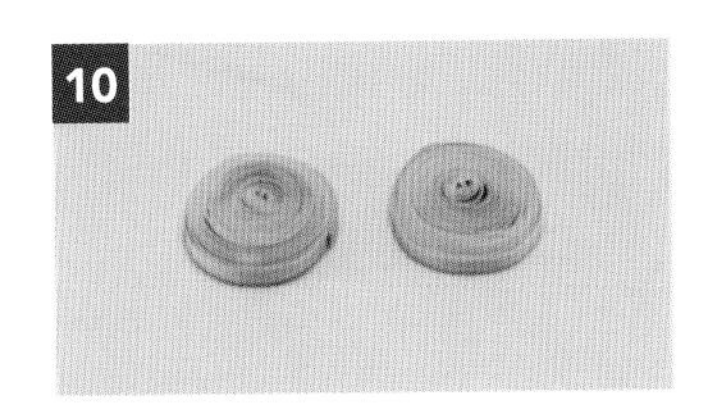

11 Glue the mouth and eyes to the head as shown in the photograph.

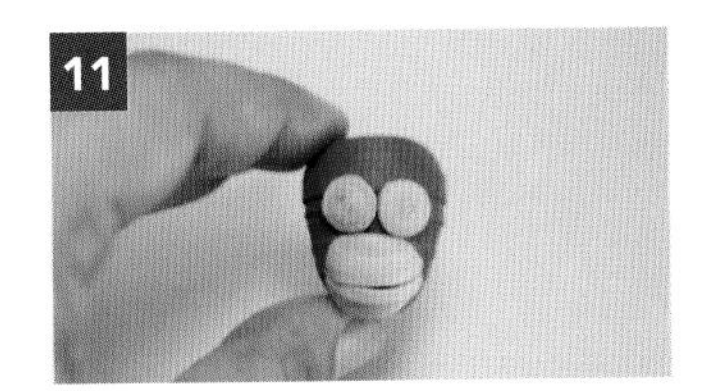

12 Cut two tapered ovals from the sheet of white paper. Cut two smaller tapered ovals from the sheet of black paper and glue to the white shapes. Glue in place to complete the eyes.

13 Quill one 1⁄32 x 11¾ in. (1 x 300mm) brown strip into a roll. Loosen the roll and glue in place.

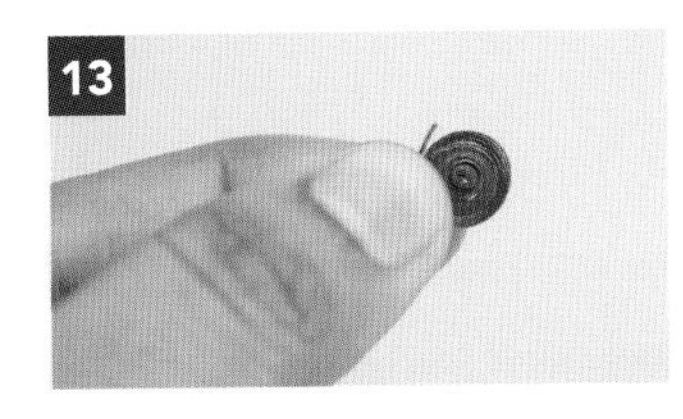

14 Press the roll into a semicircle. Glue the shape from the back. Repeat steps 13 and 14 to make a second shape.

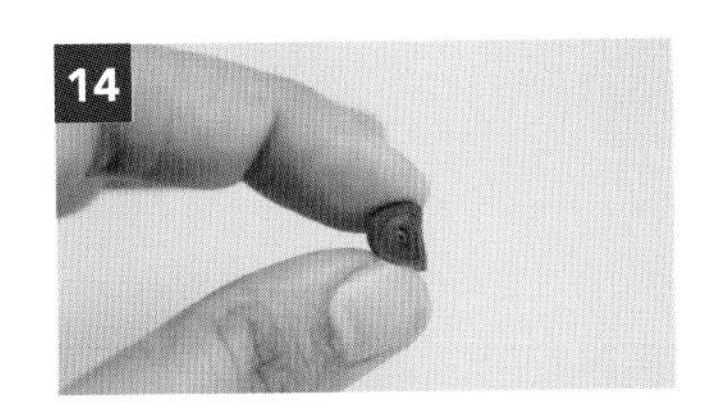

15 Glue one semicircle to each side of the head to make the ears.

Making the legs

16 Each leg is made up of three sections. Make four rolls, each using two 3⁄16 x 11¾ in. (5 x 300mm) brown strips. Use your fingers to extend it into a cone about 13⁄16 in. (30mm) high. Press two of these cones so that they are curved. Make two more rolls, each using two-and-a-half 1⁄8 x 11¾ in. (3 x 300mm) brown strips and shape them into a dome (see Techniques page 125). Glue the shapes from the inside and let dry.

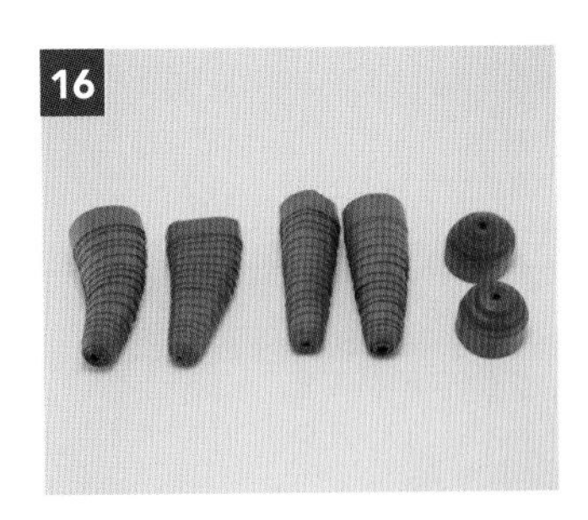

17 Glue one of the domes inside one of the curved cones. This will be an upper leg.

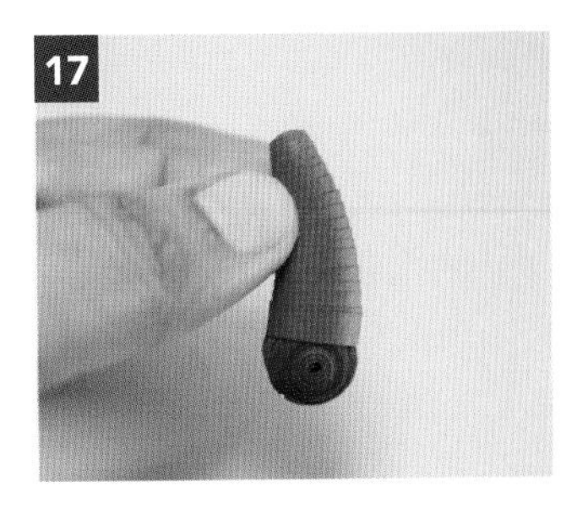

18 Press the wide end of one straight cone flat, glue this end together, then cut it into a semicircle. This will be a lower leg.

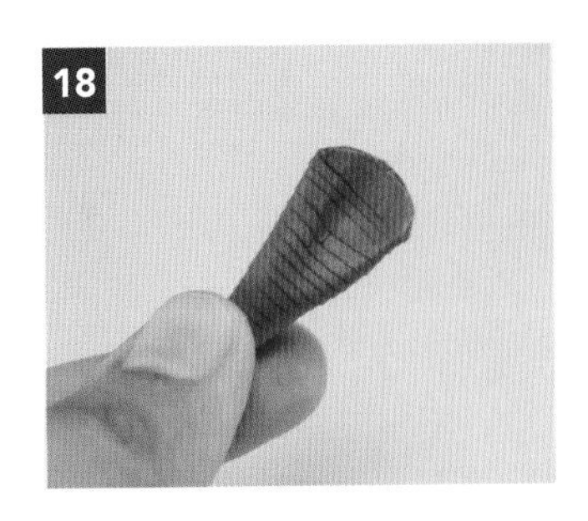

19 Glue the lower leg on the top of the curved side of the upper leg.

20 Repeat steps 17 to 19 to make the second leg, reversing the shaping as shown in the photograph.

21 Glue one leg to each side of the body, with the lower legs facing the front of the body.

22 Glue the head to the top of the body.

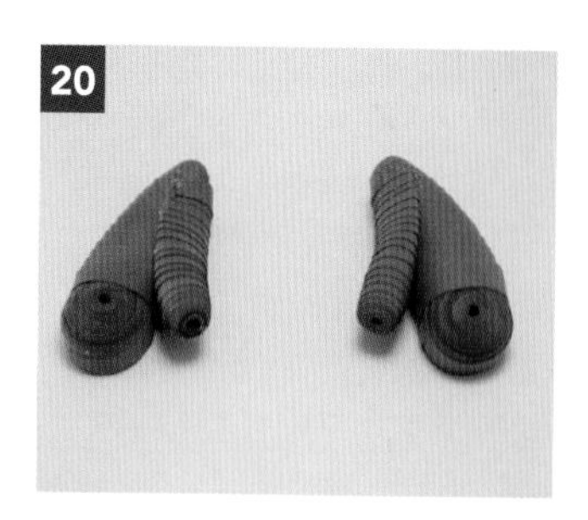

Making the arms

23 Each arm is made up of three sections. Make two rolls each using two 3/16 x 11¾ in. (5 x 300mm) brown strips. Make two more rolls each using one 3/16 x 11¾ in. (5 x 300mm) brown strip. Use your fingers to extend all four rolls into cones measuring about ¾ in. (20mm) high. Make two more rolls, each using one-and-a-half ⅛ x 11¾ in. (3 x 300mm) brown strips and shape them into a dome (see Techniques page 125). Glue the shapes from the inside and let dry.

24 Fix one dome inside one of the broader cones. This will be the upper arm. Glue the broader cone inside the narrow cone to complete the arm. Repeat to make the second arm.

25 Glue one arm to each side of the body.

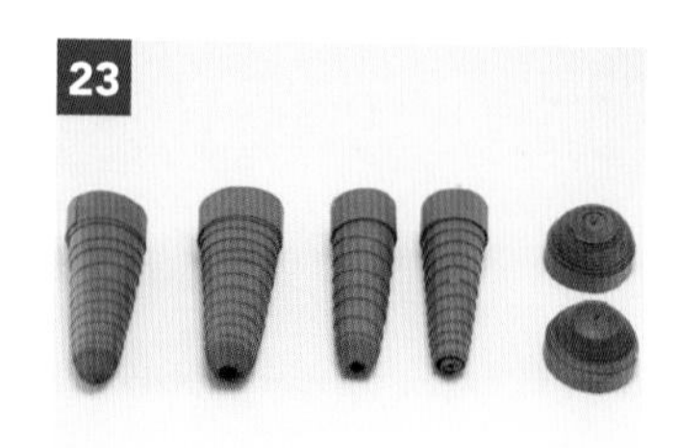

Making the tail

26 Make a roll using one ¼ x 7¾ in. (7 x 200mm) brown strip and extend it into a long cone. You can make the roll on the quilling tool, or make a tight roll and then extend it using a needle tool. Give it a slight curve then glue it from the inside. Let dry.

27 Glue the tail at the back of the body.

Making the hands and feet

28 To make the hands, make two rolls each using one ³⁄₁₆ x 6 in. (5 x 150mm) brown strip. For the feet, make two rolls each using one ³⁄₁₆ x 7¾ in. (5 x 200mm) brown strip. Extend each one into a cone ½ in. (12mm) high. Glue from the inside and let dry.

29 To make the fingers and toes, quill twenty ⅛ x 1³⁄₁₆ in. (3 x 30 mm) brown strips into thin cones directly on the quilling tool. Glue from the inside and let dry.

30 Glue five cones together and press them together at the open ends. Repeat to make four sets of five cones. Glue one set of cones to the ends of the hands and feet.

31 Glue the hands to the ends of the arms and the feet to the ends of the legs.

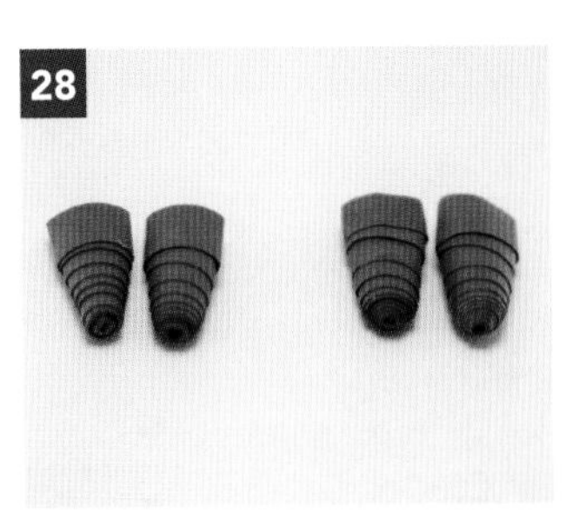

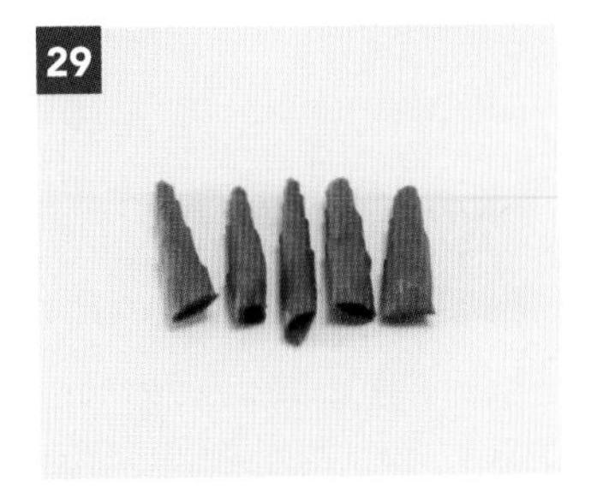

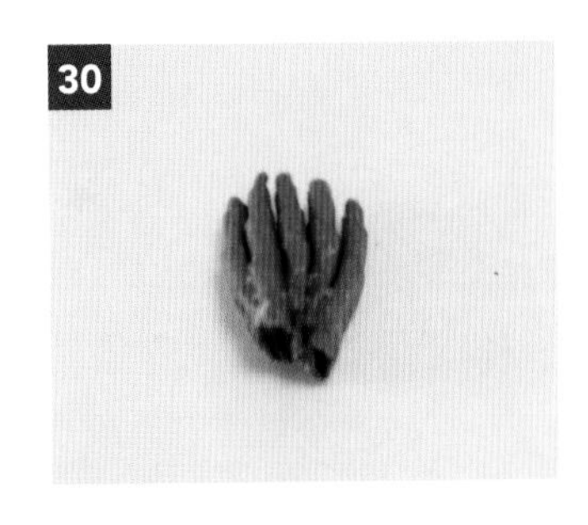

Tortoise

The tortoise, with its protective shell, symbolizes many things. It is one of the four sacred beasts in China. In ancient Greece, the god Hermes made a lyre from a tortoise shell. In India, the second time the god Vishnu was reborn he was half man and half turtle. The tortoise is the Taoist symbol of the whole universe and is said to have supported the world at the beginning of creation.

Getting started

First cut all your strips using a steel ruler and paper cutter on a cutting mat (see Techniques page 120). The tortoise has one body, one head, one shell, and four legs.

- For the body you need fifteen 1/24 x 11¾ in. (1.5 x 300mm) light brown strips
- For the head you need one ⅛ x 6 in. (3 x 150mm) and two 1/32 x 7¾ in. (1 x 200mm) light brown strips
- For the legs you need eight ⅛ x 4¾ in. (3 x 120mm) light brown strips
- For the shell you need twenty-one 1/24 x 3 in. (1.5 x 75mm), fourteen 1/24 x 11¾ in. (1.5 x 300mm), and ten 1/24 x 6 in. (1.5 x 150mm) dark brown strips; and fifteen ⅛ x 11¾ in. (3 x 300mm), twenty-eight 1/24 x 3 in. (1.5 x 75mm), seven 1/24 x 11¾ in. (1.5 x 300mm), and ten 1/24 x 6 in. (1.5 x 150mm) light brown strips
- For the eyes you need an A4 sheet of black paper

You will need

Light brown paper strips:
22 strips 1/24 x 11¾ in. (1.5 x 300mm)
1 strip ⅛ x 6 in. (3 x 150mm)
2 strips 1/32 x 7¾ in. (1 x 200mm)
8 strips ⅛ x 4¾ in. (3 x 120mm)
15 strips ⅛ x 11¾ in. (3 x 300mm)
28 strips 1/24 x 3 in. (1.5 x 75mm)
10 strips 1/24 x 6 in. (1.5 x 150mm)

Dark brown paper strips:
21 strips 1/24 x 3 in. (1.5 x 75mm)
14 strips 1/24 x 11¾ in. (1.5 x 300mm)
10 strips 1/24 x 6 in. (1.5 x 150mm)

Black paper:
1 A4-size sheet

Steel ruler
Paper cutter
Cutting mat
Quilling tool
Quilling Coach
Glue
Paintbrush
Mini Mold
Sharp pair of scissors
Paper knife
Needle tool

Finished size

Approximately 2 19/32 in. (6cm) long

Difficulty level

Easy

Making the base of the body

1 Quill fifteen $\frac{1}{24}$ x $11\frac{3}{4}$ in. (1.5 x 300mm) light brown strips to make a roll (see Techniques page 121). As you will be using a large number of narrow strips, use a Quilling Coach (see Techniques page 125).

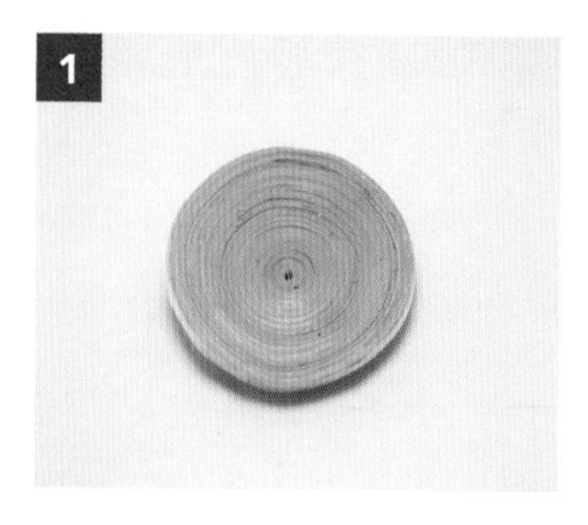

Making the head

2 Quill a roll using one $\frac{1}{8}$ x 6 in. (3 x 150mm) light brown strip. Use the tip of a paintbrush to elongate it into a cone, then use your fingers to curve it. Glue from the inside and let dry. Press the open end from two sides to flatten one side.

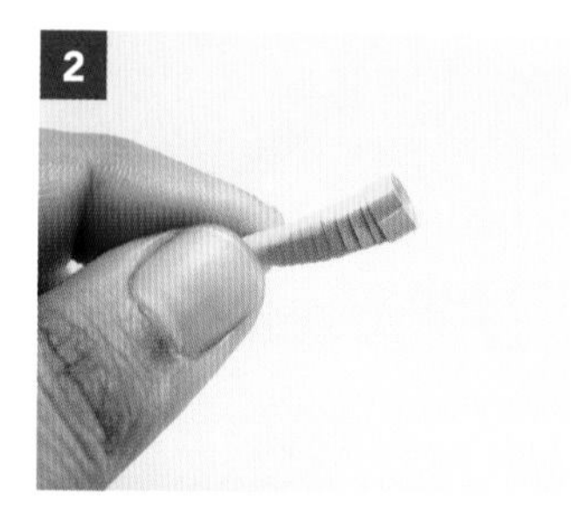

3 Make a roll using one $\frac{1}{32}$ x $7\frac{3}{4}$ in. (1 x 200mm) light brown strip. Shape it into a dome (see Techniques page 125). Glue from the inside. Make a second roll in the same way but leave it flat. Glue the back and let dry.

4 Glue the dome inside the curved end of the cone made in step 2. Glue the disk made in step 3 underneath the dome, leaving a thin gap in between them, as shown in the photograph.

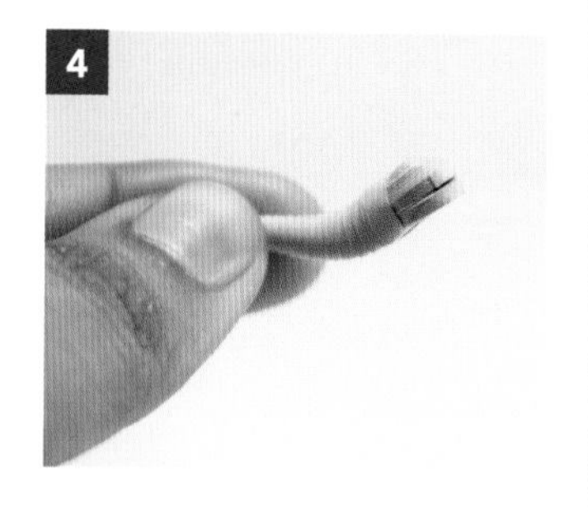

Making the legs

5 Quill one $\frac{1}{8}$ x $4\frac{3}{4}$ in. (3 x 120mm) light brown strip into a roll (see Techniques page 121) and use the tip of a paintbrush to elongate it into a cone. Use your fingers to curve the cone. Repeat step 5 to make four cones. Glue the cones from the inside and let dry.

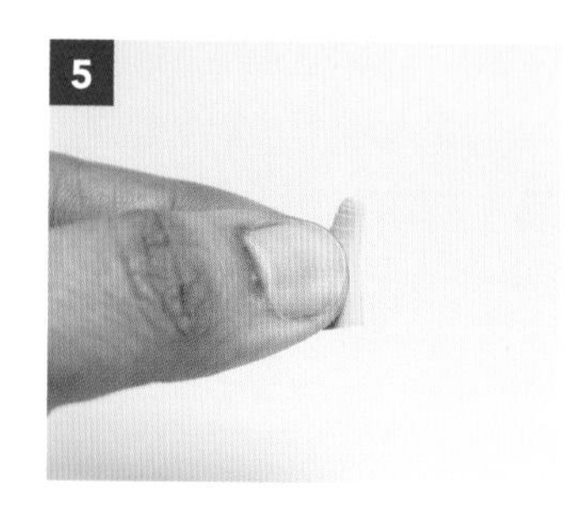

6 Make a dome using one $\frac{1}{8}$ x $4\frac{3}{4}$ in. (3 x 120mm) light brown strip. Repeat to make four domes. Glue the domes from the inside.

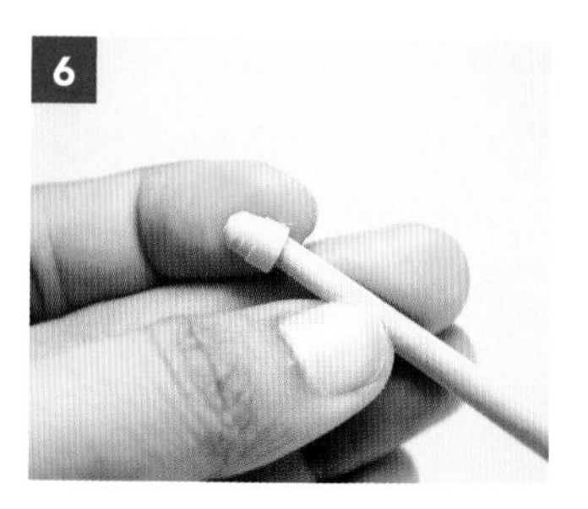

7 Glue the domes to the open ends of the curved cones made in step 5.

Assembling the base of the body

8 Flatten the back of each leg and glue them to the base of the body as shown in the photograph: two legs at the front and two at the back. Flatten the back part of the neck and glue it in between the front legs.

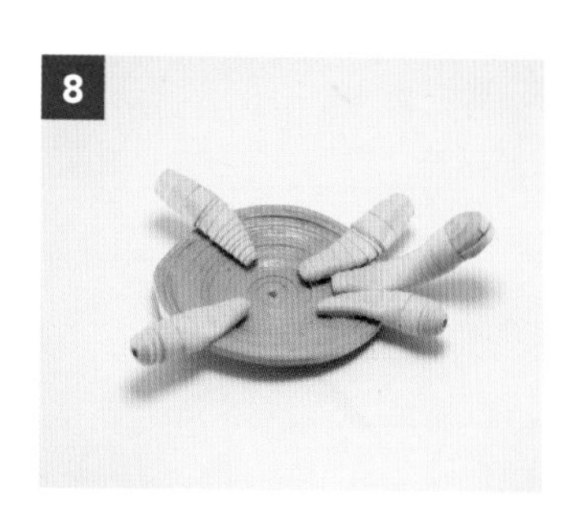

Making the shell

9 Make a roll using fifteen ⅛ x 11¾ in. (3 x 300mm) light brown strips. Shape it into a deep dome using a Mini Mold. Glue it from the inside.

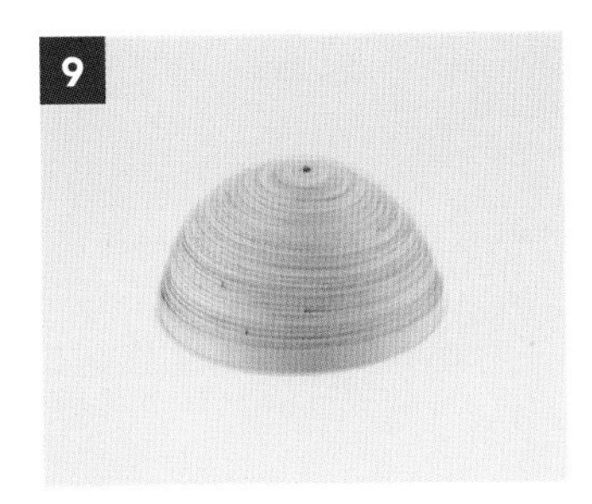

10 To make the center of the shell make seven rolls. For each roll, make a long strip by alternating four 1/24 x 3 in. (1.5 x 75mm) light brown strips and three 1/24 x 3 in. (1.5 x 75mm) dark brown strips, starting with a light brown strip (see Techniques page 121). Finish the strip with one 1/24 x 11¾ in. (1.5 x 300mm) dark brown strip. Quill this long strip into a roll and loosen it slightly so that you can press the sides (see Techniques page 121).

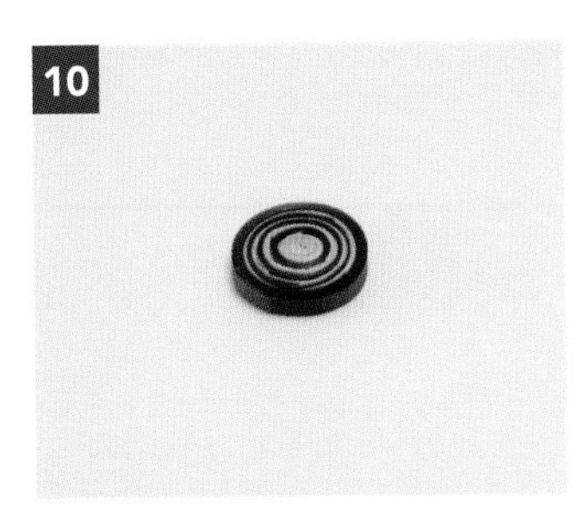

11 Use your fingers to press each roll on five sides to make a pentagon.

12 Glue the pentagons to the top of the dome made in step 9 in a flower pattern, packing them together tightly. Glue the dome to the base of the body.

13 To cover the rest of the shell you will need a number of small and large shapes. The example shown uses seven large shapes and ten small ones; use your judgment to calculate how many you need. To make a large shape, quill a roll using one 1/24 x 11¾ in. (1.5 x 300mm) light brown strip joined to one 1/24 x 11¾ in. (1.5 x 300mm) dark brown strip. Loosen the roll so that you can shape it to fit the shape of the shell. It is important that these shapes are packed together tightly. Make a total of seven pieces, each one shaped to fit a different section of the shell.

14 Glue the large shapes onto the shell to cover it. The shapes should extend below the edges of the dome to hide them and make the shell look realistic.

15 Repeat step 13 to make small shapes using one 1/24 x 6 in. (1.5 x 150mm) light brown strip and one 1/24 x 6 in. (1.5 x 150mm) dark brown strip. Make a total of ten small shapes.

16 Glue the small shapes to the sides of the dome to complete the shell. Cut two small disks from the sheet of black paper and glue to the head for the eyes.

Tools & Techniques

If you're new to quilling, you only need a few basic tools and materials: sheets of colored paper (see page 120); a paper cutter, metal ruler, and cutting mat; scissors; glue (see opposite); and a slotted quilling tool. Then, once you are ready to try some more advanced projects, you can add more items to your tool box.

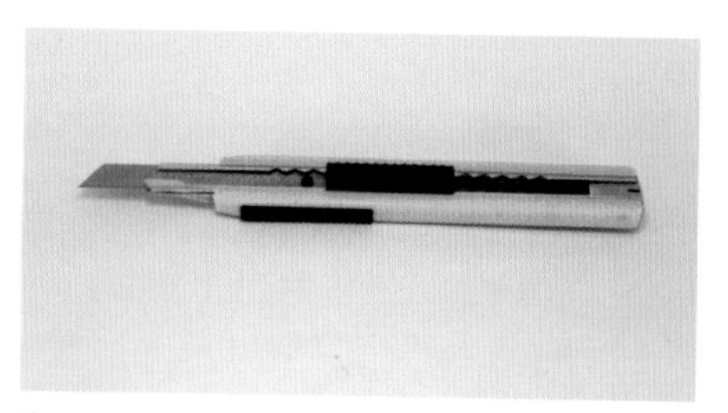

Paper cutter

Basic tools

The first step in making any quilled project is cutting the strips of paper (see page 120). To do this you will need a paper cutter, cutting mat, and metal ruler. A metal ruler is essential to guide the paper cutter—its sharp blade could cut a plastic ruler (and, possibly, your fingers). The cutting mat will protect your work surface from the cutting blade.

A sharp pair of paper scissors with straight blades is essential for cutting out shapes. A pair with curved blades will make cutting curved shapes easier, but it is not essential. You may prefer to use a paper cutting knife to cut out detailed shapes such as eyes.

You will need a quilling tool. It has a slotted tip to hold the strip of paper while you curl (quill) it into a roll (see page 121). A fine, slotted tool gives the best results. As you become more proficient you may want to quill using a needle tool. The sharp point makes it ideal for quilling small rolls, plus you can use it to apply glue to narrow areas.

Additional tools

A lot of the projects in this book use a Mini Mold (also called a dome shaper) to make dome shapes (see page 125) from your paper rolls. You can use your fingers to manipulate the paper, but a Mini Mold will help you to create neat, uniform domes.

To make petals, teardrops, and other shapes from paper rolls you allow the roll to loosen before shaping it (see page 122). You can do this by hand, or use a circle-sizing cork board.

If you are making an item that requires O-shapes (see page 124) you will need a quilling comb, which has long, straight, well-spaced teeth.

Using thin strips of paper (1/32 or 1/16 in./ 1mm or 2mm wide) to make a tight roll with a large diameter directly on a quilling tool can be fiddly. If you need to make a lot of these rolls you can use a Quilling Coach to help guide the paper strip (see page 125).

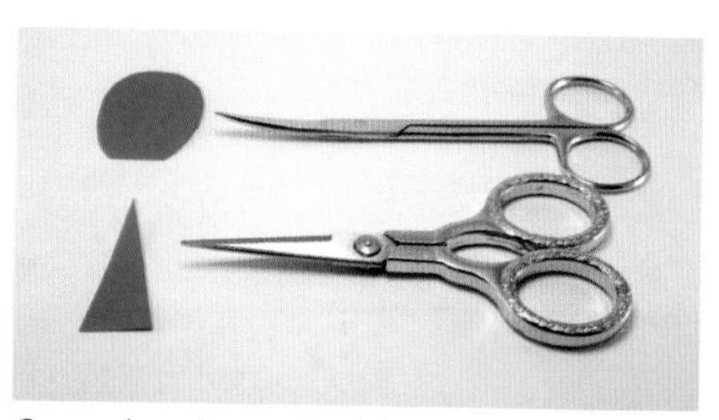

Curved and straight-bladed scissors

Quilling tool

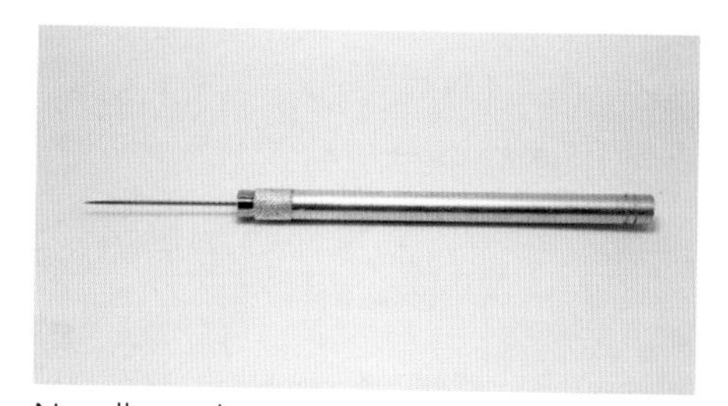

Needle tool

Some elements, such as flower petals, are embossed (raised) to help to emphasize their shape. To do this you will need an embossing pad and tool. The foam pad provides a cushion to rest the paper on while you use the tool (see page 124).

Other tools you can try include a round Border Buddy which is used to make a ring from a strip of paper (see the Sunflower, page 24); a paper crimper to crimp strips of paper (see the Dragonfly, page 62); and a circle punching machine to cut out multiple small paper disks (see the Peacock, page 86).

Additional materials

Many of the bird projects in this book use lengths of strong, flexible wire to reinforce the birds' feet. You will need a pair of wire cutters to cut the wire. The wire should be the diameter of a sewing needle and each piece should be about 3 in. (75mm) long.

If you want to give your flowers a stem, use flexible green stems sold by craft stores and online suppliers.

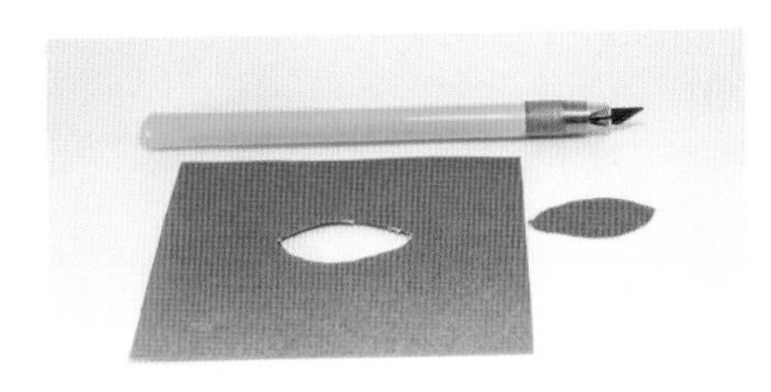

Paper cutting knife

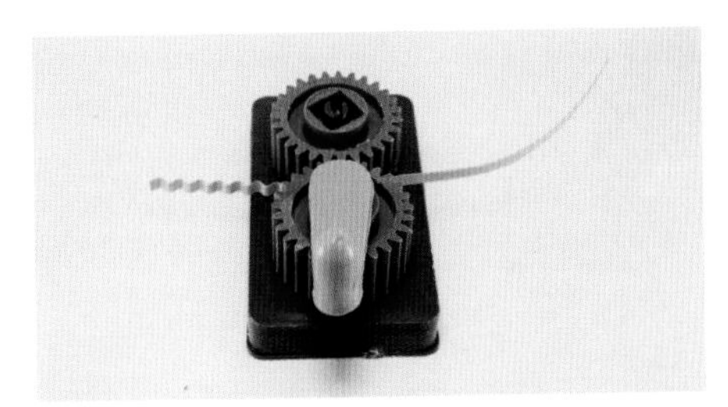

Paper crimper

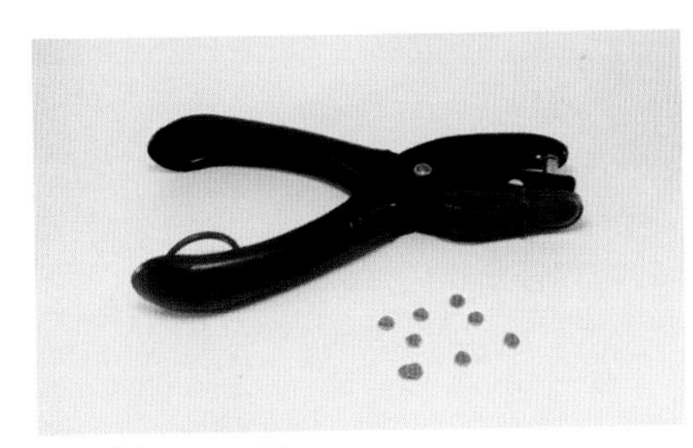

Punching machine

Glue

You can use any water-based glue to join the projects in this book.

To glue and shape the petals, mix glue and water in a ratio of two parts glue to one part water. This mixture will join the shapes without making them sticky and untidy.

Small amounts of glue will dry in a few seconds, meaning that you can continue making your project without having to wait. However, if you need to use a thick layer of glue it can take 7 or 8 hours to dry, and so you will have to wait.

Before they are joined together, apply a thick layer of glue to the back or the inside of petals, disks, domes, and cones. This ensures that they are sturdy, and the glue cannot be seen on the finished piece. Do not touch the shapes until they are completely dry or they may become distorted.

TIPS

- While the glue is drying, start to create other parts of the projects.
- Making similar shapes at the same time will save time.
- To keep your hands clean while you work—and prevent excess glue getting onto your projects—wipe them on a damp cloth while you work.

Choosing and cutting the paper

For all of the projects in this book you will need A4 sheets of colored, acid-free paper. Using acid-free paper will ensure that your projects last a long time as it is durable and will stay fresh and bright for a long time.

Paper is measured by weight —referred to by pounds or as GSM (grams per square meter). The higher the pounds or GSM, the heavier the paper will be. The weight of colored paper varies from 80 lbs to 110 lbs (120gsm to 160gsm), and the projects shown in this book were made using 100 lbs (150gsm) paper. The amount of paper required for each project is based on this weight: if you use a lighter paper you will need more strips, and if you use heavier paper you will need fewer strips.

Some of the projects require hard paper. This paper should weigh 150 lbs to 190 lbs (220gsm to 280gsm). If you cannot find paper this heavy, glue two sheets of 80 lb to 110 lb (120gsm to 160gsm) paper together and let dry. This will result in a sheet of paper that is stiff enough to use as required.

Measuring the paper strips

A sheet of A4 paper measures 8¼ x 11¹¹⁄₁₆ in. (210 x 297mm). A standard strip of paper used in this book measures 11¾ in. (300mm) but, for ease of cutting, strips cut along the 11¹¹⁄₁₆ in. (297mm) edge of a sheet of A4 can be used instead.

The easiest way to cut the strips of paper is to cut 11¾ in. (300mm) strips of the required width from an A4 sheet and then cut them into shorter lengths as necessary. To do this, remember:

- 11¾ in. (300mm) is equal to a full-length strip
- 23½ in. (600mm) is equal to two 12 in. (300mm) strips joined together (see opposite)
- 18 in. (457mm) is equal to one-and-a-half 12 in. (300mm) strips joined together (see opposite)
- 6 in. (150mm) is equal to half of one 12 in. (300mm) strip
- 3 in (75mm) is equal to one-quarter of one 12 in. (300mm) strip
- 1½ in. (37.5mm) is equal to one-eighth of one 12 in. (300mm) strip

You will have to measure other lengths, such as 8⅝ in. (220mm), 7 in. (180mm), 2⅜ in. (60mm), and ¾ in. (20mm) using a ruler.

Cutting the paper strips

To cut five strips measuring ⅛ x 11¾ in. (3 x 300mm), place a sheet of A4 paper vertically on a cutting mat. Using a pencil, mark five points at ⅛-in. (3-mm) intervals along both short edges. Place a steel ruler on the paper so that one edge joints the first set of marks. Hold the ruler firmly so that it will not slip (otherwise you will not cut a straight line). Using the edge of the ruler as a guide, use a paper cutter to cut a ⅛ x 11¾ in. (3 x 300mm) strip from the paper. Repeat to cut the remaining strips.

Safety note: The knife blade is sharp and so be aware of the position of your fingers when cutting—keep them away from the edge of the ruler while you cut the strips, and use a light pressure when cutting.

Joining the paper strips

1 To make a roll using five ⅛ x 11¾ in. (3 x 300mm) paper strips, you must start by joining the strips together to make one 57½ in. (1500mm) strip.

2 To join the strips, apply a little glue to the end of one strip. The easiest way to do this it to put a little glue on a flat surface, such as a plastic lid, so you can dip the end of the strip into it without applying too much glue.

3 Join a second strip to the glued end of the first strip so that they overlap by at least ⅛ in. (3mm).

4 Continue to attach strips in this way until they are all joined together. You can now quill the long strip into a roll.

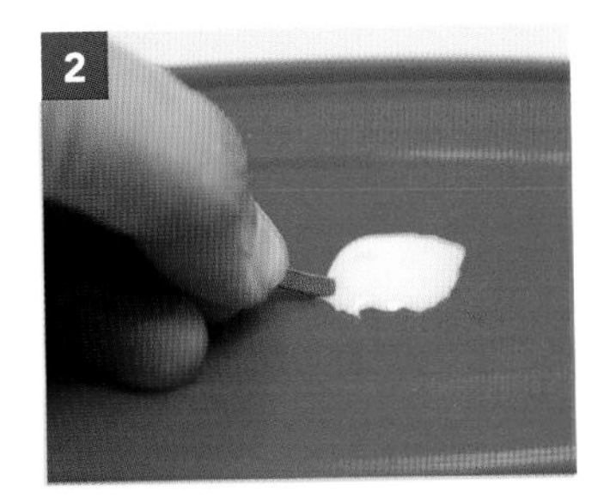

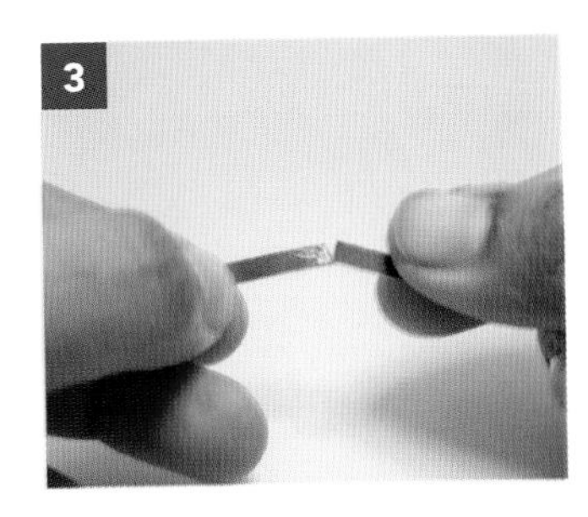

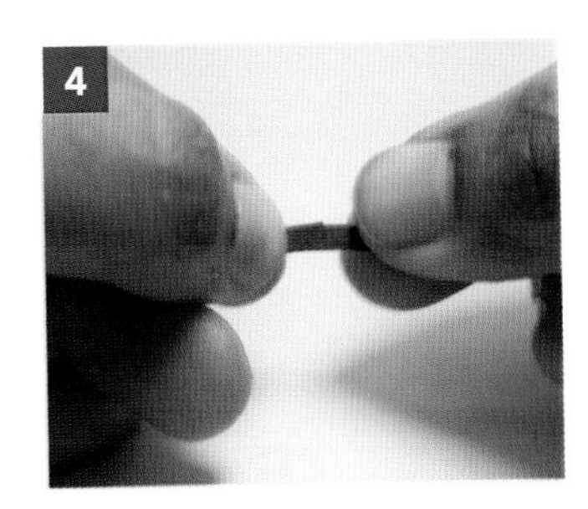

To make a tight quilled roll

Many quilled shapes start with a tight roll. Once you have mastered making these you are ready to tackle the teardrops, petals, and cones used to make the projects in this book.

1 Join the strips of paper together as required (see Joining the paper strips, left). Insert one end of the strip between the prongs of the quilling tool.

2 Roll the quilling tool so that the strip of paper curls around it to make a quill.

3 Quill the whole strip tightly, taking care not to loosen the roll and open the coils.

4 When the whole strip is quilled, remove the quilling tool and hold the roll firmly.

5 Glue the open end of the strip to the roll so that it remains tight. Use a needle tool, or a toothpick, to apply the small amount of glue required to the paper strip.

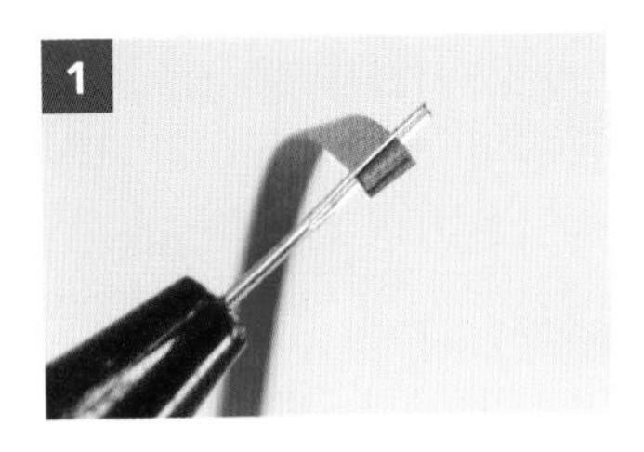

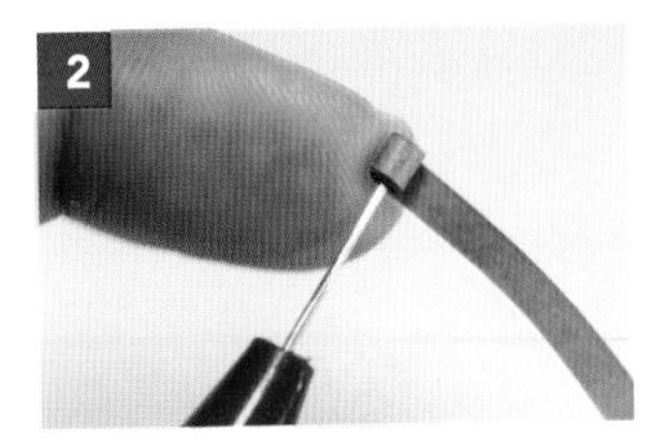

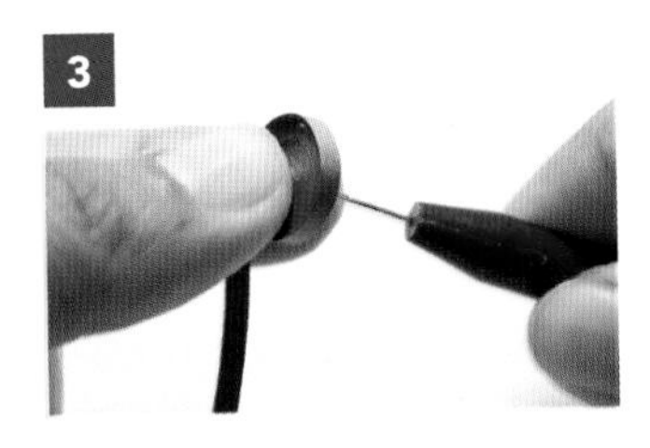

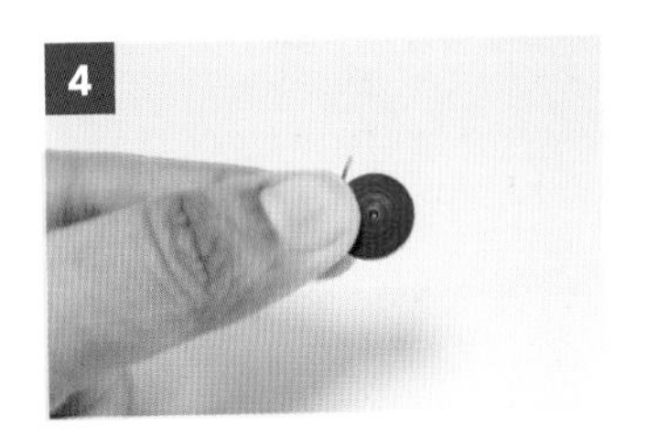

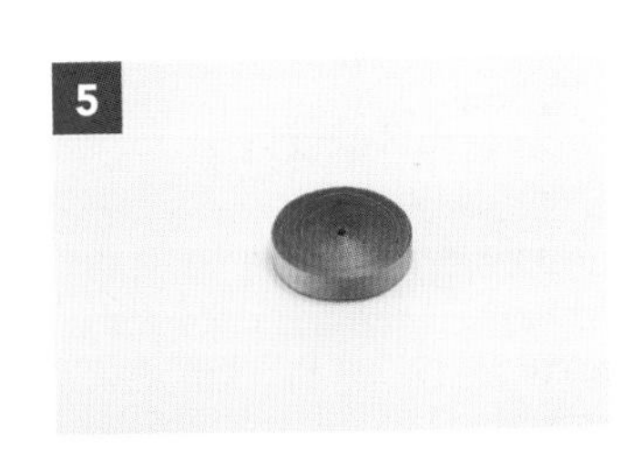

Making a teardrop

You can do this using your fingers, or with the help of a circle-sizing cork board. If your project needs multiple rolls the board will help you to ensure that all the rolls are loosened by the same amount.

1 Make a quilled roll (see page 121) but do not glue the end. Place it in one of the circles on a circle-sizing cork board. Choose the circle that is slightly larger than the quilled roll. Alternatively, loosen the roll slightly between your fingers.

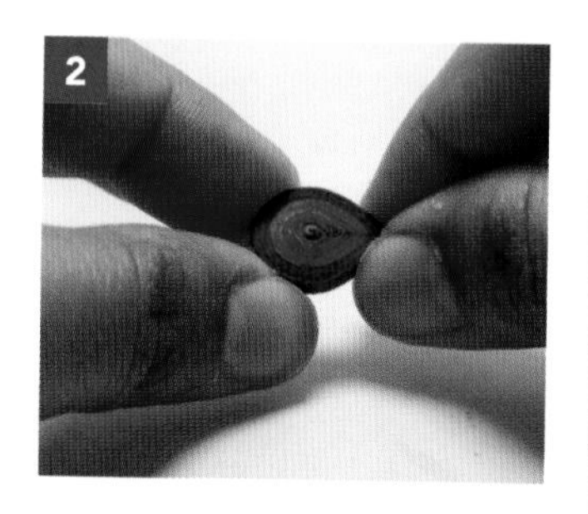

2 Remove the loosened roll from the cork board and glue the end of the strip to the roll. Use your fingers to squeeze one side of the roll to make a teardrop shape.

Making petals

You can do this using your fingers, or with the help of a circle-sizing cork board .

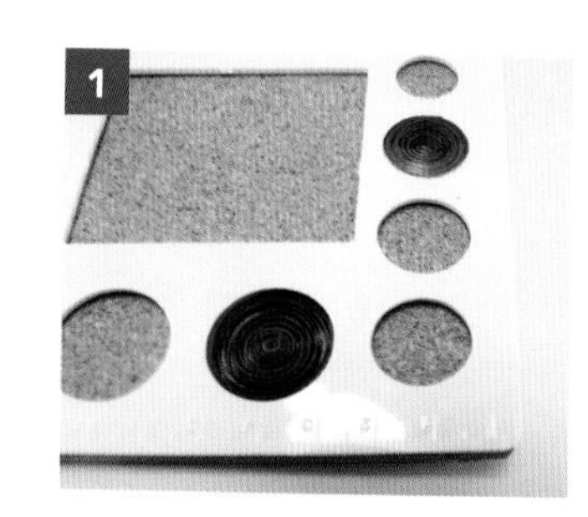

1 Make two equal-sized quilled rolls (see page 121) but do not glue the ends. For this example, the rolls have been placed in different-sized circles on a circle-sizing cork board. Loosen the rolls (they should be looser than a roll made for a teardrop): a long petal should be looser than a short petal, so use a larger hole for a long petal to allow the roll to extend further.

2 Remove the loosened rolls from the cork board and glue the ends of the strips in place.

3 Hold the center coils and then squeeze the opposite side to start to extend the shape.

4 Press the other side tightly to complete a petal shape.

5 Use a paintbrush to apply diluted glue (see page 119) to the back of the shape and let dry.

6 Before the glue is completely dry, while the paper is still pliable, press the petal so that all the coils stick together.

7 A short and a long petal are made from the same sized quilled rolls.

Cutting multiple large shapes

1 To make multiple leaves, or any item where you require several identical large shapes, fold a sheet of A4 paper in half lengthwise, then fold it a second time widthwise so you have four layers of paper.

2 Draw the leaf shapes onto the paper. You can draw the shapes freehand, or use the templates on page 126 as a guide.

3 Use a pair of scissors to cut out the shapes, cutting through all the paper layers.

4 For each shape you have drawn you will cut out four leaves.

TIP

You can fold the paper again to cut eight shapes at a time. However, if you are cutting very small shapes (see Cutting multiple small shapes, right) cutting through several layers can result in distorted shapes. In this case it is better to cut out the small shapes individually.

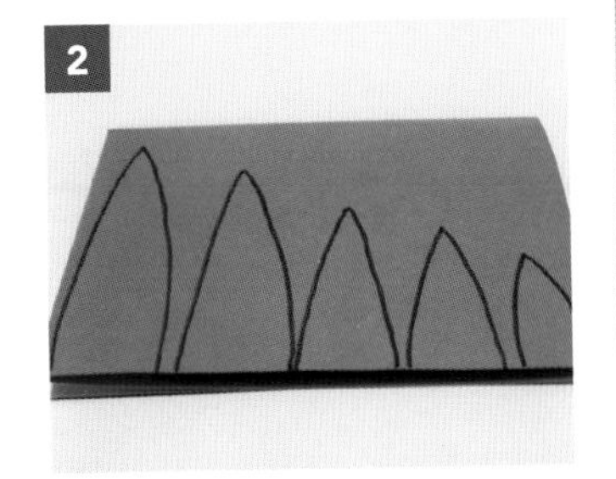

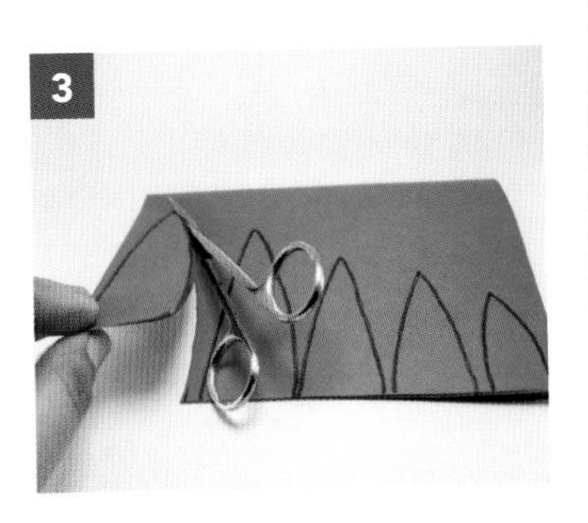

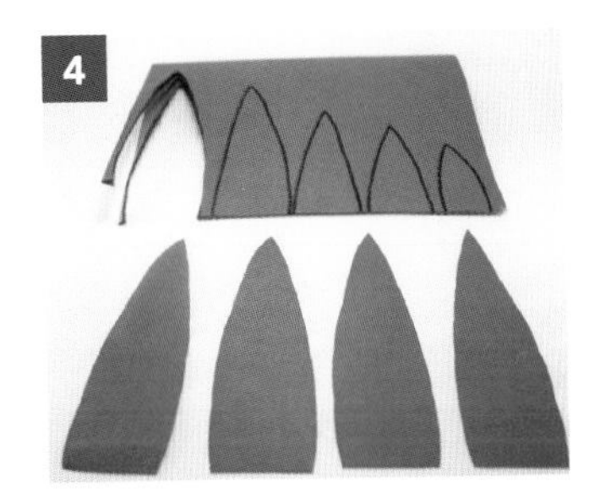

Cutting multiple small shapes

1 To make multiple feathers, or any item where you require several identical small shapes, cut strips of paper the same width as the shapes. Draw the feather shapes onto the paper. You can draw the shapes freehand, or use the templates on page 126 as a guide.

2 Use a pair of scissors to cut out the shapes one at a time.

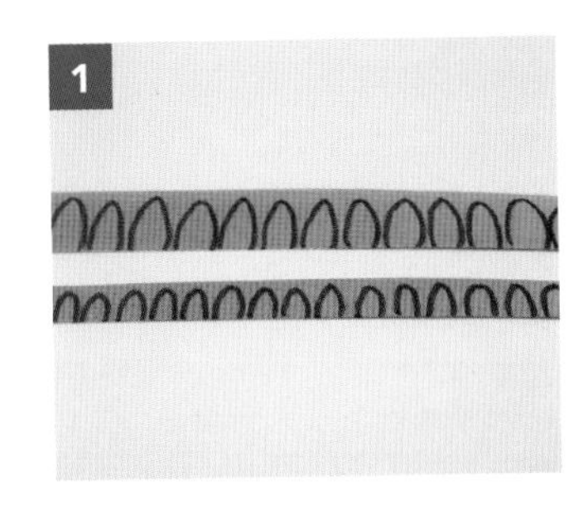

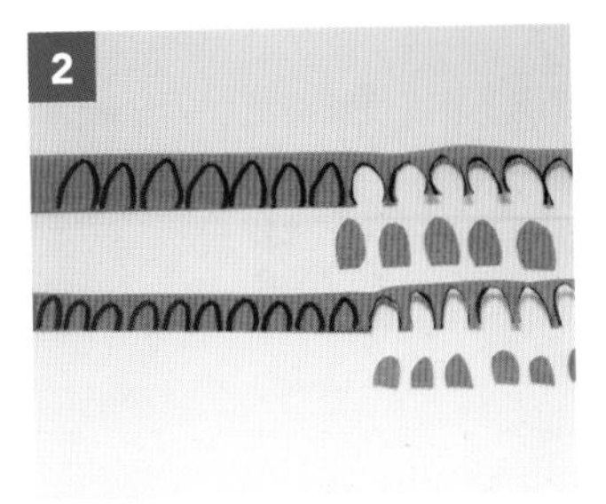

Cutting a fringe

1 To fringe a strip of paper strip, use a clip—or a series of clips—to hold one long edge of the strip of paper in place so you do not accidentally cut through it. Use a pair of scissors to cut a fringe along the length of the strip.

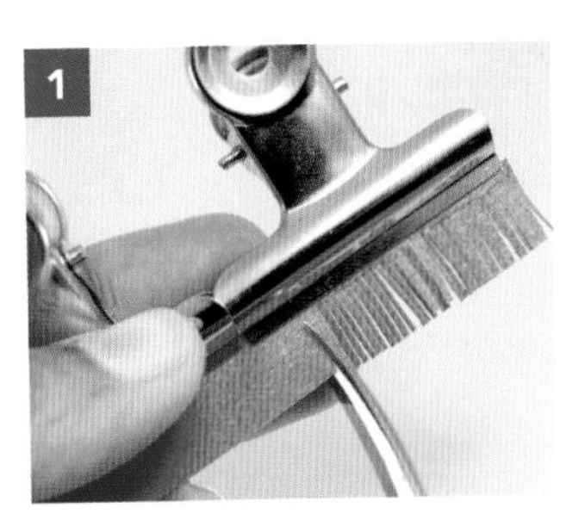

Making an O-shape

1 For this example, a ⅛ x 6 in. (3 x 150mm) strip has been used. Fold the strip 3/16 in. (5mm) from one end and place it on the seventh prong of the quilling comb so that the short end faces the front.

2 Bring the long end of the strip to the front under the eighth prong, then take it up and over the sixth prong, and finally bring it back to the front under the ninth prong.

3 Continue wrapping the strip around the comb in this way, wrapping it around the next prong each time, until you reach the fourth and eleventh prongs. Glue down the end.

4 Gently slide the coil off the comb.

5 Use your fingers to press the coil flat to form an elongated oval.

TIP

To make a larger O-shape, wrap the strip of paper around more prongs. For example, a strip measuring ⅛ x 11¾ in. (3 x 300mm) should be wrapped around the comb until you reach the second and thirteenth prongs.

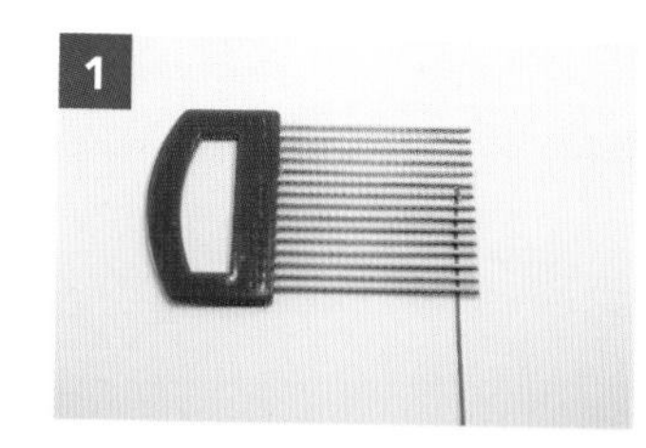
1

2

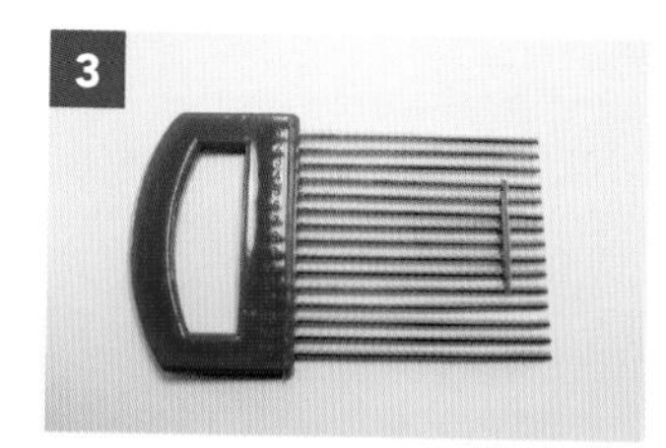
3

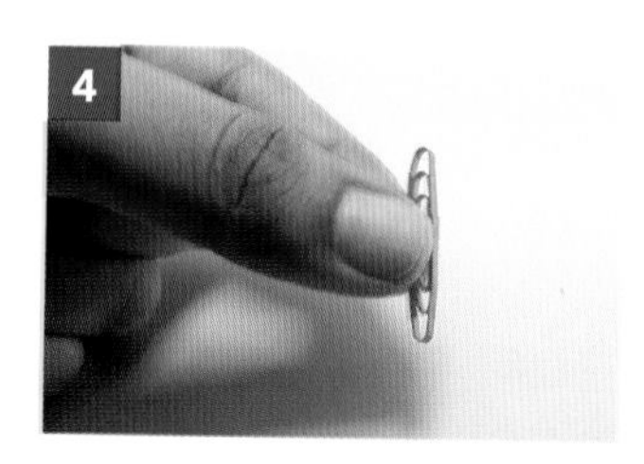
4

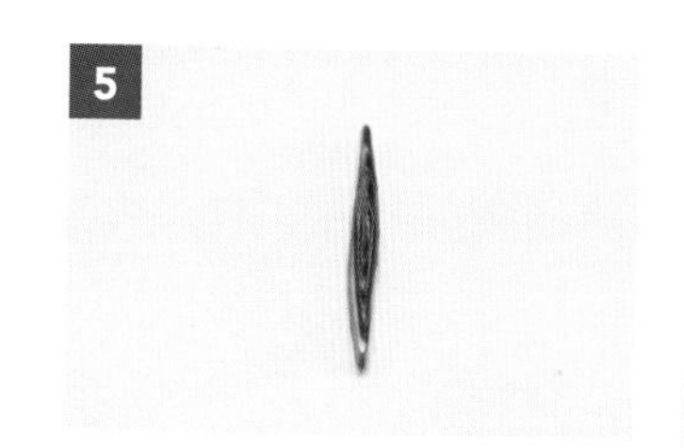
5

Making a ring

Rings can be made around a round Border Buddy, or similar cylindrical shape.

1 Glue one end of a strip of paper. Place this end of the strip of paper against the Border Buddy with the glued side facing outward (so that it does not become attached to the Border Buddy).

2 Wind the strip around the Border Buddy and attach it to the glued end. Apply glue to the entire length of the inner side of the remaining strip of paper.

3 Roll the glued paper strip around the Border Buddy to attach it to the existing paper strip. Remove the ring from the Border Buddy and use as required.

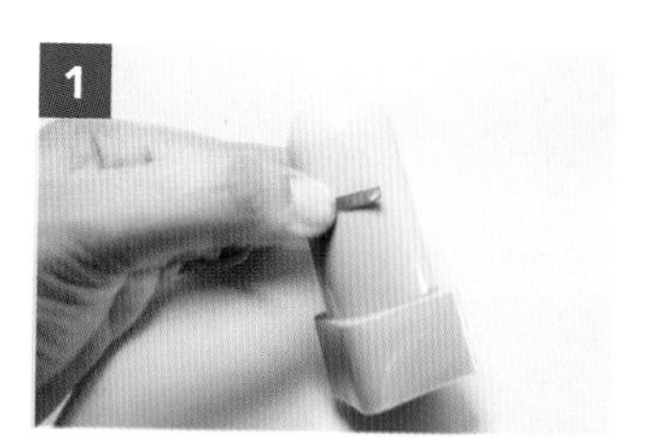
1

2

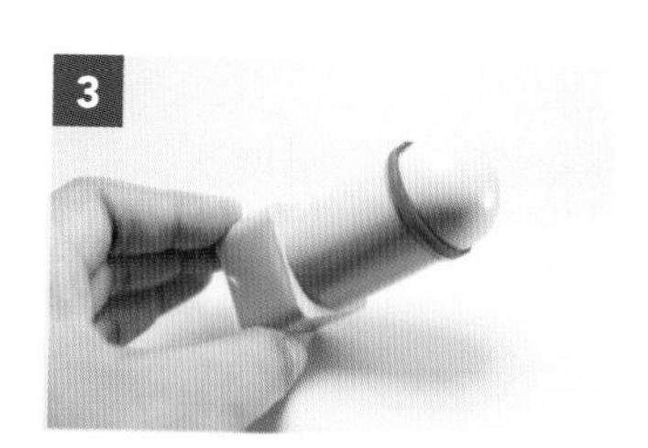
3

Using the embossing pad and tool

1 Use the embossing pad and tool to raise sections of a piece of paper. Place the paper on the foam pad to cushion it. Use the ball-shaped embossing tool to press down on the paper to raise (emboss) it.

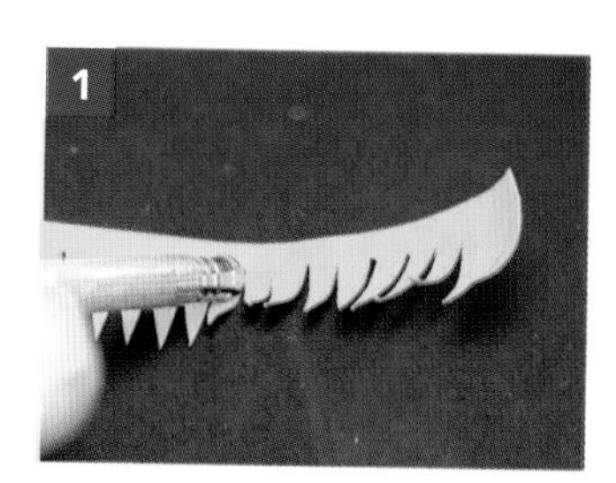
1

Making domes and cones

1 Join together ten ⅛ x 11¾ in. (3 x 300mm) paper strips and make a tight roll. Place the roll on the biggest dome of a Mini Mold. Press the roll onto the dome.

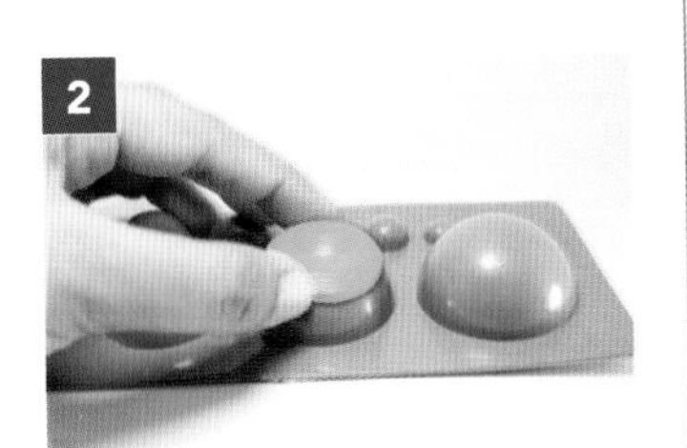

2 Move the roll to the next-biggest dome and press it onto the dome. Continue to press the roll onto larger and larger domes until you have the required shape and size.

3 To make a cone, use your fingers to manipulate the center of the dome into a point and shape it as required.

Using the Quilling Coach

A Quilling Coach is useful when you need to make a tight roll using thin strips of paper 1/32 in. or 1/16 in. (1mm or 2mm) wide.

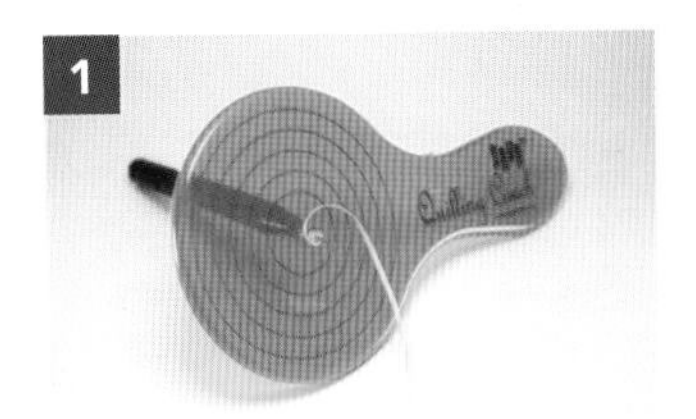

1 Insert the slots of the quilling tool in the hole in center of the Quilling Coach. Now insert the paper strip between the slots in the quilling tool and start to quill.

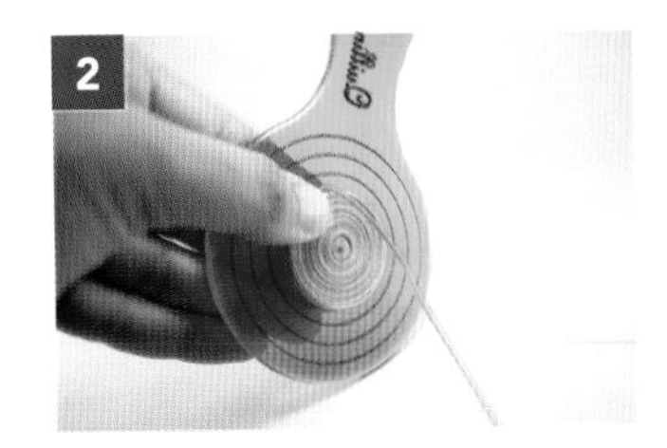

2 As the roll gets bigger, keep pressing the roll onto the base of the Quilling Coach so that it stays flat and easy to handle. Remove the quilling tool from the back of the Quilling Coach and glue the end in place.

Preserving your quilling

To keep your projects in pristine condition for as long as possible, you can seal them using a water-resistant or waterproof paper sealant. Use a flat brush to apply the sealant and make sure every coat is dry before you apply the next. Suitable sealants include:

Water-based glue. This is widely available and gives a clear, semi-glossy coat that enriches the color of paper. It is dustproof but not waterproof. Mix the glue with an equal amount of water before using it as a sealant. Use two or three coats, letting each one dry for at least 30 minutes before applying the next one.

Mod Podge. This sealant is available from craft stores and specialist online suppliers. As the name suggests, Paper Mod Podge is designed for paper and gives a smooth finish. Gloss and matte versions are available; the glossy finish has a better sheen than water-based glue.

Clear wood varnish. This sealant is available from hardware stores and should be diluted with a few drops of turpentine oil. It creates a beautiful shine and gloss. Used on its own it has a yellowish tint; to avoid this apply two coats of water-based glue before using the varnish. For the best results, use a minimum of three coats of varnish, allowing at least 1 hour for each one to dry.

Acrylic sprays. A number of acrylic sprays with gloss and matte finishes are available. They are designed to stiffen the paper and dry quickly. Read the package instructions before use and test the spray on a sample of paper before using it on a finished project.

Templates

Lotus Leaf
Photocopy at 400 percent to enlarge it to full size.

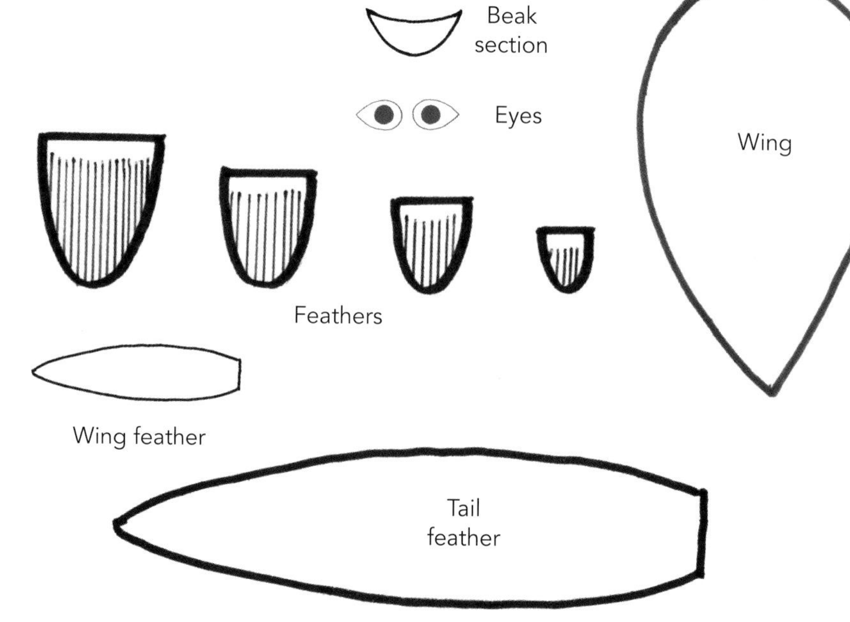

Parrot
Photocopy at 100 percent.

Pineapple Leaves
Photocopy at 450 percent to enlarge them to full size.

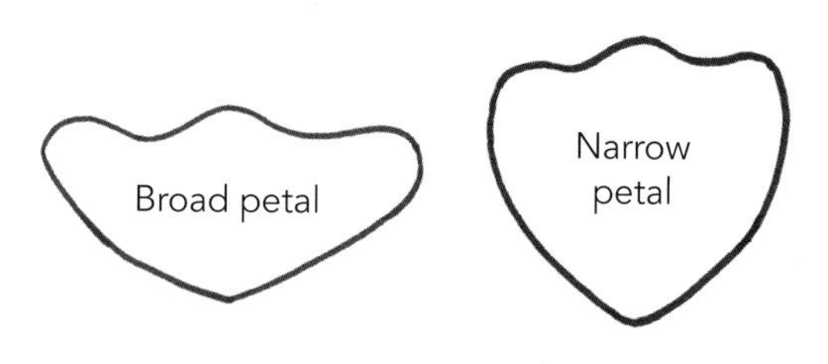

Poppy Petals
Photocopy the petals at 200 percent to enlarge them to full size.

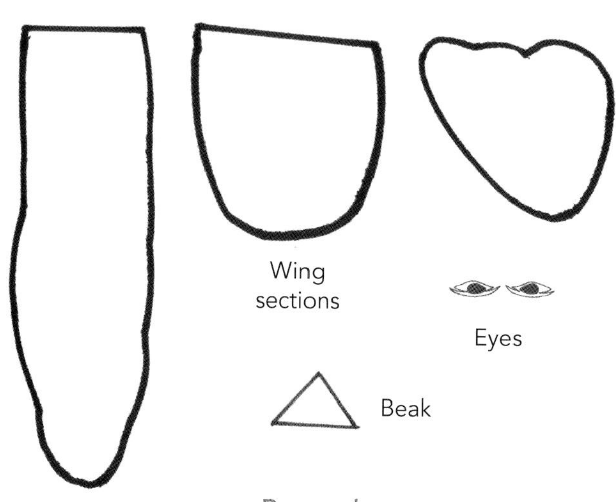

Peacock
Photocopy at 100 percent.

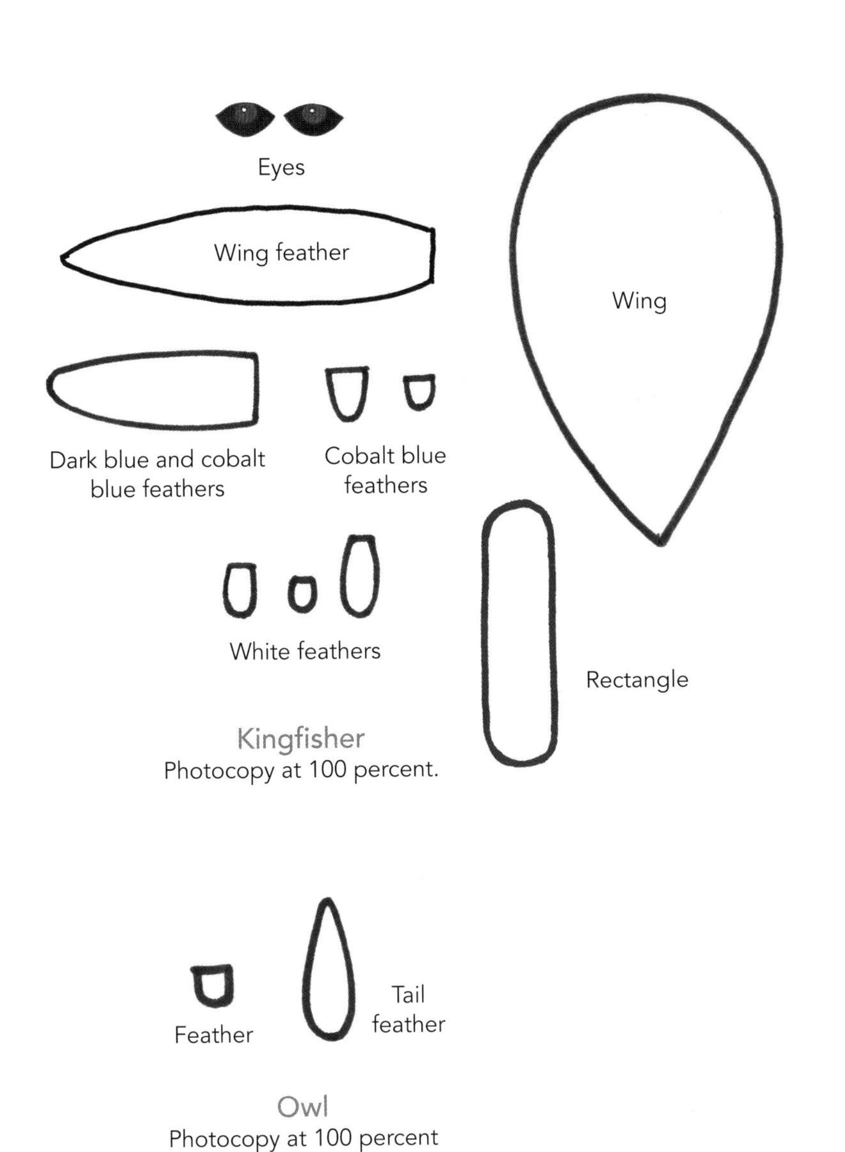

Kingfisher

Photocopy at 100 percent.

Owl

Photocopy at 100 percent

Lion

Photocopy at 50 percent to reduce them to full size.

Butterfly Wing

Photocopy at 200 percent to enlarge it to full size.

Elephant

Photocopy at 50 percent to reduce them to full size.

Monkey

Photocopy at 50 percent to reduce them to full size.

Tortoise

Photocopy at 50 percent to reduce them to full size.

Index

Resources

Amazon
amazon.com

Blick Art Materials
dickblick.com

Custom Quilling Supplies
customquillingbydenise.com

Hobby Lobby
hobbylobby.com

Jo-Ann Fabric and Craft Stores
joann.com

Lake City Craft Company
quilling.com

Little Circles
littlecirclesshop.net

Michaels
michaels.com

Quill On
letsquillon.com

Quilled Creations
quilledcreations.com

Quilling Superstore
quillingsuperstore.com

Quilling Supply
quillingsupply.com